# 100 FABULOUS
# CAKES
## AND
# TORTES

# 100 FABULOUS

# CAKES

## AND

# TORTES

*Exotic and delightful
recipes, icings, toppings
and decorations*

◆

# AARON MAREE

**Angus&Robertson**
An imprint of HarperCollins*Publishers*

First published in Australia as *Cakes, Tortes and Gateaux of the World* in 1991
by CollinsAngus&Robertson
A Division of HarperCollins Publishers (Australia) Pty Limited
25 Ryde Road, Pymble, Sydney NSW 2073, Australia

This edition published in 1995

Distributed in the US by
**HarperCollins World**
10 East 53rd Street, New York NY 10022–5299

National Library of Australia Cataloguing-in-Publication data:

Maree Aaron
[Cakes, tortes and gâteaux of the world].
100 fabulous cakes and tortes.

Includes index.
ISBN 0 207 18870 X (pbk)
1. Cake.  I. Title.  II Title: One hundred fabulous cakes and tortes.
III. Title: Cakes, tortes and gateaux of the world.
641.8653

Printed in Hong Kong

9 8 7 6 5 4 3 2 1     95  96  97  98  99

# CONTENTS

*This book is dedicated to my teachers who have taught me all I know and to my good friend and assistant, Angela C. Jarvis.*

## ACKNOWLEDGEMENTS

The author would like to thank the following people and organisations for their assistance and support:

Waterford Wedgwood Australia Limited

Perry Snodgrass Catering

Dianna Dasey

John R. Sexton, senior lecturer, College of Tourism and Hospitality, Coorparoo, Brisbane

Mrs J. Curry, home economics teacher, Tasmania

Robert Fischer, American Society of Bakery Engineers, USA

P.A.T. Foods and their Carma range of products

Kenwood Appliances Australia

Defiance Milling, Queensland

My publisher Pam Brewster

Socomin International Fine Foods and their Odense range of products

Trumps Nuts and Dried Fruits, Brisbane

NSW Egg Producers Co-operative Limited

Special thanks to John Dart, Brian Cox, David Watson and Helen Cramp who kindly supplied the ingredients used to produce the cakes for this book

# INTRODUCTION

Cakes that turn every day into a special occasion should tantalize the eye without necessarily requiring elaborate assembly or detailed decoration. The cakes in this book will grace a family meal or honour special guests. Some recipes are not for the faint-hearted or busy cook but for those who enjoy a baking indulgence. More difficult recipes include step-by-step instructions so don't be afraid to extend your culinary skills.

The tempting treats in Layers of Sweetness combine a variety of fillings and toppings with layers of cake including the traditional génoise — a featherlight sponge designed to complement rich fillings — and japonaise — a versatile meringue-style base. Enhance any occasion with the richness of a Coconut Cake or highlight a special table setting with the vibrant yellow of a Mimosa Torte.

Classic Fare includes traditional cakes from around the world any cook will be proud to perfect. Triumph with an American Pineapple Upside Down Cake — originally adapted from the classic French Tarte Tatin — or serve a timeless High Tea Cake. This chapter includes cakes from Hungary and Vienna as well as the more familiar German tortes.

You will never have to ask them twice if you offer the melt-in-the-mouth marzipan and pastry of Golden Moments. Offer the almond-rich Pithiviers from a tiny village south of Paris. The Austrian Linzer Torte combines almonds and rich pastry with the tang of red currant jam.

Create the perfect dessert with something Light and Luscious like the Chocolate Delice — for true chocolate fanatics with white and dark chocolate smothering a sweet almond base. For something stronger, try the coffee liqueur flavoured Tirami-sù.

Richly Rustic offers the cook a choice of yeast cakes from around the world. The brioche style Kulich with its peel and fruit or the rich rum syrup of the French Savarin will warm any winter day.

Enhance your cakes with Toppings and Fillings for a professional look. Follow the recipes as written or experiment to perfect exotic adaptations of your own. Some cakes will work with a minimum of decoration — some yeast cakes need little accompaniment — while others — like the japonaise or génoise bases — are made to be decorated. Whichever you choose, remember that these cakes are made to be eaten!

# LAYERS *of* SWEETNESS

## Layered, filled and rolled cakes

## DOBOS TORTE

*This torte was invented by Josef Dobos to commemorate the National Hungarian Exhibition of 1885. The caramel topping is a little tricky so be prepared to work quickly when cutting the caramel wedges.*

**8 egg yolks**
**120 g (4 ¹/₄ oz) icing (powdered) sugar**
**8 egg whites**
**120 g (4 ¹/₄ oz) icing (powdered) sugar, extra**
**180 g (6 ¹/₄ oz) plain (all-purpose) flour**

FILLING
**250 g (9 oz) unsalted butter**
**75 g (2 ¹/₂ oz) cocoa powder**
**120 g (4 ¹/₄ oz) dark (plain or semi-sweet) chocolate,**
**melted (see page 159)**
**75 g (2 ¹/₂ oz) cornflour (cornstarch)**
**100 ml (3 ¹/₂ fl oz) milk**
**5 egg yolks**
**460 ml (16 fl oz) milk, extra**
**320 g (11 ¹/₄ oz) caster (superfine) sugar**

TOPPING
**200 g (7 oz) caster (superfine) sugar**
**30 g (1 oz) unsalted butter**
**flaked almonds, roasted for decoration (see page 171)**

Preheat oven to 180 deg C (350 deg F). Line five baking trays (sheets) with baking parchment and draw a 23 cm (9 in) circle on each.

Beat the egg yolks and icing sugar for about 20 minutes or until thick and fluffy. Beat the egg whites until stiff peaks form (see page 173), then beat in the extra icing sugar, a spoonful at a time. Sift the flour onto the beaten egg yolks. Spoon the beaten egg whites onto the mixture then very gently fold in by hand. Spread the mixture evenly into the five circles on the prepared trays and bake in the preheated oven for 5–8 minutes or until lightly browned and the top of each cake springs back when lightly touched. Turn the cakes out onto wire racks to cool.

FILLING
Cream the butter until light, fluffy and almost white. Beat in the cocoa and melted chocolate.

Blend the cornflour, 100 ml of milk and egg yolks. Place the extra milk in a saucepan and bring to the boil, stir in the sugar and then pour into the egg yolk mixture, stirring all the time. Return the mixture to the saucepan and cook for 2 minutes or until thickened, stirring all the time. Cool. When completely cold, beat into the chocolate mixture.

TOPPING
Place the sugar in a heavy saucepan and heat until it melts and caramelizes, stirring occasionally. Add the

butter and stir until melted and mixed, then pour onto one of the cakes. Spread the caramel quickly and evenly and while it is still soft, cut into 12 equal wedges with a hot, oiled, sharp knife.

### To Assemble

Spread the cooled filling over the remaining cakes, reserving sufficient filling to cover the sides, and stack one on top of the other. Cover the sides with the filling mixture and place the caramel-topped wedges on the top. Press flaked almonds around the sides. Cut the cake into 12, each portion topped with a caramel wedge, and serve immediately.

**STEP THREE:** *Take another layer of cake and spread a quarter of the cooled filling over the top.*

**STEP ONE:** *Melt the sugar in a saucepan and add the butter when the sugar is dissolved and golden brown in colour. When the butter is melted and mixed, pour the caramel onto one of the cakes.*

**STEP FOUR:** *Top with a layer of sponge spread with the filling. Repeat until all the layers of sponge are used.*

**STEP TWO:** *Spread the caramel quickly and evenly. Allow this to cool slightly. While the caramel is still soft use a hot, oiled knife to cut the disc into 12 wedges. This must be done quickly.*

**STEP FIVE:** *Cover the top and sides of the cake with the remaining filling. Press almonds around the side. Place the caramel-topped wedges on the top of the cake. Serve immediately.*

# COCONUT CAKE

*This soft moist cake is for the growing number of coconut fanatics who crave its rich sweet flavour.*

*100 ml (3 ¹/₂ fl oz) coconut cream*
*200 g (7 oz) caster (superfine) sugar*
*60 ml (2 fl oz) rum*
*400 g (14 oz) desiccated (flaked) coconut*
*100 ml (3 ¹/₂ fl oz) milk*
*50 g (1 ³/₄ oz) cornflour (cornstarch)*
*3 egg yolks*
*480 ml (17 fl oz) milk, extra*
*3 egg whites*
*90 g (3 oz) caster (superfine) sugar, extra*
*1 vanilla génoise sponge (see page 58)*
*shredded coconut, extra for decorating*

Place the coconut cream, sugar and rum in a saucepan and bring to the boil. Pour over the coconut and allow to soak for one hour.

Blend 100 ml of milk with the cornflour and egg yolks. Place the remaining milk in a saucepan and bring to the boil. Pour onto the cornflour and egg mixture, beating all the time. Return the mixture to the saucepan and cook for 2 minutes, stirring all the time. Keep custard mixture warm. Beat the egg whites until stiff peaks form (see page 173), then gradually beat in the extra sugar a spoonful at a time. Fold into the warm custard.

Cut the sponge horizontally into thirds. Spread the bottom layer with half of the soaked coconut and spoon on one third of the custard. Top with a layer of sponge. Repeat with the remaining coconut and another third of the custard. Top with a layer of sponge. Cover the top and sides of the cake with the remaining custard and the shredded coconut.

# MIMOSA TORTE

*L*ike *the sunny yellow colour of Australian wattle, or mimosa, this cake is named for its yolk-yellow interior and bright yellow marzipan decoration.*

**235 g (8 ¼ oz) cornflour (cornstarch)**
**130 g (4 ½ oz) plain (all-purpose) flour**
**6 egg yolks**
**6 x 60 g (2 oz, large) eggs**
**130 g (4 ½ oz) caster (superfine) sugar**
**45 g (1 ½ oz) honey**

### TO DECORATE
**1 quantity quick no-fuss buttercream (see page 156)**
**125 g (4 ½ oz) marzipan, tinted yellow (see page 169)**
**icing (powdered) sugar for dusting**
**60 ml (2 fl oz) dark (plain or semi-sweet) chocolate, melted (see page 159)**

Preheat oven to 180 deg C (350 deg F). Grease two 23 cm (9 in) spring form pans lightly with butter and line the bases with baking parchment. Mix the flours and sift twice.

Beat the egg yolks, eggs and sugar until light and fluffy and the mixture forms a ribbon (see page 172). Stir in the honey and gently fold in by hand the sifted flours.

Pour the mixture into prepared pans and bake for 40 minutes or until the top of each cake springs back when lightly touched. Cool in the pans on a wire rack.

When cold, cut one cake horizontally into thirds. Spread the buttercream on each layer and stack one on top of the other. Cover the top and sides with more buttercream. Roll out the marzipan into a 10 cm (4 in) circle and place in the centre of the top layer. For extra effect, texture the marzipan with a patterned rolling pin.

Cut the second cake into 2 cm (³/₄ in) cubes and place randomly around the marzipan and on the sides of the cake. Dust lightly with icing sugar. Decorate with piped chocolate.

**STEP ONE:** *Cover the filled and layered cake with buttercream.*

**STEP TWO:** *Place the yellow marzipan in the centre on top of the cake.*

**STEP THREE:** *Cover the rest of the cake top with 2 cm (³/₄ in) cubes of cake. Decorate.*

# TRIO TORTE

This torte has three different creams sandwiched between layers of meringue. It is a very rich torte so only serve thin slices.

**3 japonaise bases, use 1 ¹/₂ quantity
(see page 57)**

### VANILLA CREAM
**220 ml (7 ³/₄ fl oz) thickened (double or heavy) cream
40 g (1 ¹/₂ oz) icing (powdered) sugar
50 g (1 ³/₄ oz) white chocolate, chopped
60 g (2 oz) unsalted butter, melted**

### MILK CHOCOLATE CREAM
**220 ml (7 ³/₄ fl oz) thickened (double or heavy) cream
40 g (1 ¹/₂ oz) icing (powdered) sugar
60 g (2 oz) unsalted butter, melted
100 g (3 ¹/₂ oz) milk chocolate**

### CHOCOLATE CREAM
**220 ml (7 ³/₄ fl oz) thickened (double or heavy) cream
300 g (10 ¹/₂ oz) dark (plain or semi-sweet) chocolate, chopped**

**cocoa powder for dusting**

The method is exactly the same for all the cream fillings.

Place the cream into a saucepan and bring to the boil. Add the remaining ingredients and stir until mixed. Chill. When cold, whip the cream until stiff.

Spread vanilla cream over one japonaise base. Top with a second base. Spread top with the milk chocolate cream and top with the remaining base. Cover the top and sides of the torte with chocolate cream. Chill for one hour and dust with cocoa powder.

# NAPOLITAIN

$T$*his Italian inspired torte has crisp biscuit-like rounds of rich sweet pastry, sandwiched together with strawberry jam and coated with a fondant glaze.*

510 g (18 oz) plain (all-purpose) flour
380 g (13 ¹/₂ oz) unsalted butter, cut into small pieces
180 g (6 ¹/₄ oz) ground almonds
180 g (6 ¹/₄ oz) caster (superfine) sugar
3 x 60 g (2 oz, large) eggs
1 egg yolk
grated rind of 2 lemons
200 g (7 oz) strawberry jam
250 g (9 oz) fondant glaze (see page 166)
60 g (2 oz) dark (plain or semi-sweet) chocolate, melted (see page 159)
1 quantity ganache (see page 164)

Place the flour, butter, ground almonds and sugar in a bowl and very lightly rub in the butter until the mixture resembles coarse breadcrumbs. Add the eggs, egg yolk and grated rind to make a firm dough. Wrap the dough in plastic (cling) wrap and chill for one hour.

Preheat the oven to 180 deg C (350 deg F). Line three baking trays (sheets) with baking parchment.

Roll out the chilled dough thinly (it may seem dry and crumbly but can be rolled after a little kneading) and cut three 23 cm (9 in) circles. Place on the prepared trays and bake in the preheated oven for 8–10 minutes. Cool in the trays on wire racks.

When cool cover two of the pastries with strawberry jam and stack them one on top of the other and top with the remaining pastry. Pour three quarters of the heated fondant over the top of the torte and allow a little to drizzle down the sides. Colour the remaining fondant with melted chocolate and pipe fine lines across the cake. Using a tooth-pick, feather the chocolate into the white fondant (see page 168). Pipe around the edge with ganache.

# PYRAMID CAKE

I*t won't take as long to make this cake as it took the Egyptians to build the pyramids but the result is equally impressive.*

### CAKE

*60 g (2 oz) plain (all-purpose) flour*
*60 g (2 oz) cornflour (cornstarch)*
*150 g (5 1/4 oz) unsalted butter*
*90 g (3 oz) caster (superfine) sugar*
*60 g (2 oz) marzipan (see page 168), finely chopped*
*7 egg yolks*
*8 egg whites*
*100 g (3 1/2 oz) caster (superfine) sugar, extra*
*30 g (1 oz) ground almonds*

### FILLING

*200 ml (7 fl oz) cream (single or light)*
*20 g (3/4 oz) unsalted butter*
*600 g (21 oz) dark (plain or semi-sweet) chocolate, chopped*
*cocoa powder for dusting*

Preheat oven to 180 deg C (350 deg F). Line three 28 cm x 20 cm (11 in x 8 in) baking trays (sheets) with baking parchment. Mix the flours and sift twice.

Beat the butter, sugar and marzipan until creamy, light and fluffy. Add the egg yolks one at a time, beating very well after each one is added. Beat the egg whites until stiff peaks form (see page 173), then add the extra sugar a spoonful at a time. Beat until the sugar is dissolved. Gently fold in by hand the sifted flour and ground almonds, then the beaten marzipan mixture. Spread the mixture onto the prepared trays and bake for 15–20 minutes or until the top of each cake springs back when lightly touched and the cakes have shrunk slightly away from the sides of the trays. Cool on the trays for 5 minutes before turning out onto wire racks to cool.

### FILLING

Place the cream and butter in a saucepan and bring to the boil. Remove from the heat and quickly stir in the chopped chocolate. Stir until the chocolate is melted. Chill. Stir occasionally so that no lumps form. Do not allow the filling to become too thick. It must remain easy to spread.

### TO ASSEMBLE

Cut the cakes into 7 cm (2 3/4 in) strips and spread thinly with the chocolate. Stack on top of each other until the pile is 7 cm (2 3/4 in) high. Chill for 30 minutes.

Place the chilled cake on the very edge of the bench top (countertop). Place a ruler along the top edge of the cake furthest from you and cut diagonally through to the bottom edge nearest you with a clean serrated knife. The ruler and bench top edge are used to guide the knife. When cut, you will have two triangles of cake.

Stand the triangles so that the layers of cake run vertically. Join the two triangles together to make a pyramid shape with a thin layer of chocolate mixture.

Cover the two sloping sides with the chocolate mixture and chill for 30 minutes. Dust with the cocoa powder.

**STEP ONE:** *Remove the baked cake sheet from its tray and remove the baking parchment. Cut the cake into 7 cm (2 3/4 in) strips.*

**STEP TWO:** *Cover the first of the strips with the chocolate filling and place the next strip on top. Cover this evenly with the filling. Continue adding cake strips and chocolate filling until the stack is approximately 7 cm (2 3/4 in) high. Chill for 30 minutes.*

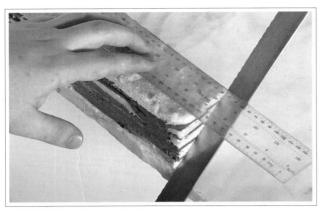

**STEP THREE:** *Place the chilled stack on the very edge of the work bench and place a ruler along the top edge of the cake furthest from you. Cut diagonally along the bottom edge nearest you with a clean serrated knife. The ruler and the bench top edge are used as the guide for the knife.*

**STEP FIVE:** *Join the two triangles together with a thin layer of the chocolate mixture to form a pyramid, ensuring that all the layers are running in the same direction.*

**STEP FOUR:** *When cut you will have two triangles of cake. Stand the triangles so that the layers run vertically.*

**STEP SIX:** *To finish the cake, cover the two sloping edges with chocolate mixture and chill for a further 30 minutes. When chilled dust with cocoa powder and serve.*

# LEMON SHORTCAKE

This tangy lemon cake is simple, easy and quick to make. It is also delicious.

370 g (13 oz) plain (all-purpose) flour
3 level teaspoons baking powder
125 g (4 ¹/₂ oz) salted butter
125 g (4 ¹/₂ oz) caster (superfine) sugar
4 x 60 g (2 oz, large) eggs

FILLING
grated rind and juice of 2 lemons
100 g (3 ¹/₂ oz) unsalted butter
125 g (4 ¹/₂ oz) icing (powdered) sugar
lemon rind, grated for decoration

Preheat oven to 180 deg C (350 deg F). Grease a 23 cm (9 in) spring form pan very lightly with butter and line the base with baking parchment. Sift the flour and baking powder.

Beat the butter and sugar until creamy, light and fluffy. Add the eggs one at a time, beating very well after each one is added. Gently mix in by hand the sifted flour and baking powder. Do not over mix. Pour into the prepared pan and bake for 45–50 minutes or until the cake has shrunk slightly away from the sides of the pan and a skewer inserted into the centre of the cake comes out dry. Cool in the pan on a wire rack.

FILLING
Beat the lemon rind and juice with the butter until creamy. Beat in sufficient icing sugar to make a stiff icing.

When the cake is cold cut in half horizontally. Spread the top of one layer with three quarters of the filling. Top with the second layer. Cover the top and sides of the cake with reserved filling. Decorate with lemon rind.

# CHERRY DOME TORTE

$F$*orget about spreading the buttercream evenly to achieve a perfectly flat finish. Pile the buttercream into the centre of each layer to give this cake its distinctive dome shape.*

*¹/₂ vanilla génoise sponge (cut horizontally)
(see page 58)*
*¹/₂ chocolate génoise sponge (cut horizontally)
(see page 59)*
*1 quantity quick no-fuss vanilla buttercream
(see page 156)*
*200 g (7 oz) maraschino cherries, drained and
chopped*

### TO DECORATE
*300 g (10 ¹/₂ oz) marzipan (see page 168)*
*300 g (10 ¹/₂ oz) dark (plain or semi-sweet) chocolate,
melted (see page 159)*
*icing (powdered) sugar for dusting or marzipan flowers
(see page 170)*

Cut each sponge into halves horizontally. Cover the layers of sponge with the vanilla buttercream. Place cherries in the centre of each layer and cover with a mound of buttercream. Stack, in alternating layers, the chocolate and vanilla cake. Mould the cake to give the dome shape.

Cover top and the sides thickly with the remaining buttercream. Chill for 30 minutes. Roll out the marzipan and cover the top and the sides. Paint on the chocolate with a pastry brush. Dust cake lightly with icing sugar or decorate with marzipan flowers. Chill for one hour before serving.

**STEP ONE:** *Make each layer of sponge dome slightly in the centre by spreading the buttercream thicker in the middle and adding the cherries to the centre.*

**STEP TWO:** *When all the layers are joined together, cover the top and sides with buttercream. Cover the dome with marzipan.*

**STEP THREE:** *When the marzipan has been moulded to the sides of the torte and any excess has been removed, paint the top and sides with melted chocolate.*

# BLACK FOREST GÂTEAU

*Named after the majestic Black Forest in Germany, it has become one of the world's best known cakes. Everyone loves the flavour of the Kirsch liqueur and sour cherries.*

### BASE
*100 g (3 ¹/₂ oz) plain (all-purpose) flour*
*45 g (1 ¹/₂ oz) icing (powdered) sugar*
*60 g (2 oz) unsalted butter, softened*
*1 x 60 g (2 oz, large) egg*
*2 teaspoons water*

*1 chocolate génoise sponge (see page 59), cut into quarters horizontally*

### FILLING
*500 ml ( 17 ¹/₂ fl oz) crème Chantilly (see page 164)*
*400 g (14 oz) canned sour black cherries, drained and pitted*
*60 ml (2 fl oz) Kirsch*

### TO DECORATE
*crème Chantilly (reserved)*
*chocolate curls (see page 162)*
*icing (powdered) sugar for dusting*
*12 glacé (candied) cherries*

Place the flour and icing sugar in a bowl and very lightly rub in the butter until the mixture resembles coarse breadcrumbs. Add the egg and sufficient water to make a firm dough. Wrap the dough in plastic (cling) wrap and chill for one hour.

Preheat oven to 180 deg C (350 deg F). Grease the base of a 23 cm (9 in) spring form pan lightly with butter and roll out the chilled dough to fit the prepared base. Bake for 5–10 minutes or until light golden brown. Cool.

### TO ASSEMBLE
Reserve a quarter of the crème Chantilly for decorating. Spread the cooled pastry base with a small amount of the crème Chantilly. Place one of the sponge cake layers on top. Spread with a quarter of the crème Chantilly, cover with some of the cherries and sprinkle on a little of the Kirsch. Repeat this until all but one of the sponge layers have been used. Top with the remaining sponge layer.

Cover the top and sides with the remaining crème Chantilly. Decorate the cake with chocolate curls. Lightly dust with icing sugar and position the glacé cherries around the edge. Chill.

Remove from the refrigerator 10–15 minutes before serving.

**STEP ONE:** *Layer each slice of sponge with crème Chantilly and sour black cherries. Sprinkle with Kirsch.*

**STEP TWO:** *When all of the sponge layers have been filled and layered on top of each other, cover the top and sides of the cake with more crème Chantilly.*

**STEP THREE:** *Decorate with chocolate curls, icing sugar and glacé cherries.*

# FRENCH ALMOND TORTE

$T$*his torte, made with feathery light almond meringue layers and milk chocolate mousse, is very rich and very memorable.*

*200 g (7 oz) marzipan*
*200 ml (7 fl oz) milk*
*60 g (2 oz) plain (all-purpose) flour* mistake
*5 egg whites* + egg yolks
*200 g (7 oz) caster (superfine) sugar*

FILLING
*600 ml (21 fl oz) cream (single or light)*
*600 g (21 oz) dark (plain or semi-sweet) chocolate, chopped finely*
*5 egg yolks, lightly beaten* EGG SUBS!
*4 egg whites* cooked
*100 g (3 ¹/₂ oz) caster (superfine) sugar, extra*

TO DECORATE
*icing (powdered) sugar for dusting*
*200 g (7 oz) flaked almonds, roasted (see page 171)*

Preheat oven to 200 deg C (400 deg F). Line four baking trays (sheets) with baking parchment and draw 23 cm (9 in) circles on each.

Place the marzipan and milk in a saucepan and bring slowly to the boil, stirring all the time. Cook until the mixture thickens and there are no lumps. Add the flour and cook until the mixture is thick and smooth, stirring all the time. Cool slightly.

Beat the egg whites until stiff peaks form (see page 173) then gradually beat in the sugar a spoonful at a time. Beat until the sugar is dissolved. Take a spoonful of the egg white mixture and mix by hand into the marzipan mixture. Gently fold in the remaining egg white mixture. Place a quarter of the mixture in the centre of each circle and spread evenly to the edges. Bake for 30 minutes. Cool on the trays on wire racks.

FILLING
Heat the cream in a small saucepan and bring to the boil. Remove from the heat and add the chocolate. Stir until the chocolate is melted. Mix the egg yolks into the chocolate and cream. Chill until cool and thickened. Beat the egg whites until stiff peaks form then gradually beat in the sugar a spoonful at a time. Beat until the sugar is dissolved. Take a spoonful of

the egg white mixture and mix by hand into the cooled chocolate mixture. Gently fold in the remaining egg white mixture.

TO ASSEMBLE
Place one of the baked marzipan circles on the base of a 23 cm (9 in) spring form pan and pour on one third of the filling. Repeat with the remaining layers. Gently press down on the top layer to evenly spread the filling. Freeze for one hour.

Before serving dust the torte with icing sugar and press flaked almonds around the side.

**STEP ONE:** *Carefully fold the egg whites into the chocolate mixture and pour a quarter of the filling onto the first layer of cake.*

**STEP TWO:** *Continue alternating the filling with layers of cake until all are used. Place the last layer of cake on top and chill the torte for one hour.*

# DUTCH APPLE TORTE

*This torte combines two distinctive flavours — almonds and tart apples — in a casing of rich sweet shortbread. It's a treat to eat.*

### BASE
*300 g (10 ½ oz) plain (all-purpose) flour*
*150 g (5 ¼ oz) icing (powdered) sugar*
*200 g (7 oz) unsalted butter, cut into small pieces*
*2 x 60 g (2 oz, large) eggs, lightly beaten*
*30 ml (1 fl oz) water*

*100 g (3 ½ oz) apricot jam*
*½ vanilla génoise sponge, cut horizontally*
*(see page 58)*

### FILLING
*5 cooking apples, cored and thinly sliced*
*6 level teaspoons ground cinnamon*
*30 ml (1 fl oz) Calvados*
*100 g (3 ½ oz) sugar*
*50 g (1 ¾ oz) ground almonds*
*100 g (3 ½ oz) desiccated (flaked) coconut*

### TO DECORATE
*200 g (7 oz) apricot glaze (see page 166)*
*200 g (7 oz) fondant, melted (see page 166)*
*100 g (3 ½ oz) flaked almonds, roasted (see page 171)*

Preheat oven to 200 deg C (400 deg F). Grease a 23 cm (9 in) spring form pan lightly with butter and line the base with baking parchment.

Place the flour and icing sugar in a bowl. Add the butter and very lightly rub into the flour and icing sugar until the mixture resembles fresh bread-crumbs. Add the eggs and sufficient water to make a firm dough. Knead several times to ensure that all ingredients are thoroughly blended. Wrap in plastic (cling) wrap and chill for 30 minutes.

Combine all the filling ingredients.

### TO ASSEMBLE
Roll out the chilled pastry into a circle large enough to cover the base and sides of the prepared pan. Ease the pastry into place and trim the edges. Spread the base with apricot jam and top with a layer of sponge. Spoon on the apple filling. Roll out the remaining pastry and cut to cover the top. Press and seal the edges. Bake for 30–35 minutes. Cool in the pan on a wire rack. Remove the spring form rim when the torte is lukewarm. Brush the top and sides with the apricot glaze and allow to dry. Brush glaze with melted fondant and allow to dry. Press roasted almonds around the top edges.

**STEP ONE:** *Place the layer of sponge on the base of the pastry lined tin.*

**STEP TWO:** *Fill the centre of the pastry with the apple filling and press down so that it is even with the top of the tin.*

**STEP THREE:** *Cover the top of the torte with thinly rolled pastry.*

# PISCHINGER TORTE

*In this rich chocolate torte, hazelnuts replace the almonds more usual in the japonaise bases.*

*500 g (17 ¹/₂ oz) quick no-fuss chocolate buttercream (see page 156)*
*200 g (7 oz) praline, crushed (see page 158)*
*2 japonaise bases made with ground hazelnuts (see page 57)*
*1 chocolate génoise sponge (see page 59), either whole or cut horizontally into two layers*
*400 g (14 oz) hazelnuts, halved*
*icing (powdered) sugar, for dusting*

Mix together the chocolate buttercream and the praline and spread some onto one of the japonaise bases. Place the génoise layer on top and spread with the buttercream and praline mixture. Top with the remaining japonaise base. If using two layers of génoise sponge, place one of the génoise layers on top of the japonaise base and spread with the buttercream and praline mixture. Repeat with the second cake layer. Top with the remaining japonaise base.

Trim the edges of the torte so that the cake and meringue layers are even. Cover the top and sides with the remaining buttercream. Press halved hazelnuts into the side of the cake. Dust with icing sugar. Chill for 20 minutes.

**STEP ONE:** *Cover the base with buttercream and place the chocolate sponge layer on top. Cover with more buttercream.*

**STEP TWO:** *Place the second japonaise base on top of the sponge.*

**STEP THREE:** *Cover the whole cake with chocolate buttercream and decorate with halved hazelnuts.*

# CHOCOLATE HERRISON TORTE

*Another one for the chocoholics. To achieve the spiky hedgehog effect, pile the filling in the centre and flick the chocolate coating lightly with a knife.*

### BASE
*100 g (3 ¹/₂ oz) plain (all-purpose) flour*
*45 g (1 ¹/₂ ) icing (powdered) sugar*
*60 g (2 oz) unsalted butter, softened*
*1 x 60 g (2 oz, large) egg*
*2 teaspoons water*
*strawberry jam*

### GANACHE TOPPING
*250 ml (9 fl oz) cream (single or light)*
*600 g (21 oz) dark (plain or semi-sweet) chocolate, chopped*
*1 chocolate génoise sponge (see page 59)*
*1 quantity of crème chiboust (see page 164)*
*cocoa powder for dusting*

Place the flour and icing sugar in a bowl and very lightly rub in the butter until the mixture resembles coarse breadcrumbs. Add the egg and sufficient water to make a firm dough. Wrap the dough in plastic (cling) wrap and chill for one hour.

Preheat oven to 180 deg C (350 deg F). Grease the base of a 23 cm (9in) spring form pan lightly with butter and roll out the chilled dough to fit the prepared base. Bake for 5–10 minutes or until the top is a light golden brown. Cool.

Place the cream in a saucepan and bring to the boil. Remove from the heat and add the chocolate. Stir until the chocolate is melted and the mixture looks silken and shiny. Chill for 2 hours, stirring every now and then to make sure the mixture is not setting completely hard. After 2 hours beat for 15 minutes or until light, fluffy and pale in colour.

### TO ASSEMBLE
Spread the cooled pastry with the warm jam. Cut the sponge into thirds horizontally. Place a layer of sponge onto the base and spread with three quarters of the crème chiboust, leaving a mound in the centre to make a dome shape. Place the next layer of sponge on the dome and press down around the edges to ensure the sponge is firmly fixed. Spread with remaining créme chiboust domed in the centre.

Place the last layer of sponge on top and press down around the edges as before. Chill the torte for one hour and cover with the beaten ganache topping. Flick topping with a knife to achieve a spiky finish.

Dust with cocoa powder and chill for 30 minutes before serving.

**STEP ONE:** *Place the first layer of sponge onto the jam-covered pastry base. Spread the crème chiboust, making it slightly domed in the centre.*

**STEP TWO:** *Continue layering each slice of sponge with crème chiboust domed in the centre.*

**STEP THREE:** *Cover the outside of the cake with ganache and flick with a palette knife to give a spiky look.*

# INDONESIAN LAYER CAKE

*In this multi-layered cake half of the butter, sugar and egg mixture is not included in the baked cake but used as a buttercream to fill and coat the finished cake.*

*60 g (2 oz) plain (all-purpose) flour*
*45 g (1 ¹/₂ oz) cornflour (cornstarch)*
*300 g (10 ¹/₂ oz) unsalted butter*
*100 g (3 ¹/₂ oz) caster (superfine) sugar*
*8 egg yolks*
*8 egg whites*
*100 g (3 ¹/₂ oz) caster (superfine) sugar, extra*
*2 level teaspoons instant coffee*
*3 teaspoons hot water*

TO DECORATE
*125 g (4 ¹/₂ oz) flaked almonds, roasted*
*(see page 171)*
*icing (powdered) sugar for dusting*

Preheat oven to 180 deg C (350 deg F). Line four 20 cm x 30 cm (8 in x 12 in) baking trays (sheets) with baking parchment. Mix the flours and sift twice.

Beat the butter and sugar until creamy, light and fluffy.

Add the egg yolks, one at a time, beating very well after each one is added. Beat the egg whites until stiff peaks form (see page 173), then gradually beat in the extra sugar a spoonful at a time. Beat until the sugar is dissolved. Gently fold in by hand the sifted flours and half of the creamed butter and sugar. Reserve the other half of the creamed butter and sugar for the filling. Divide the cake mixture in half. Leave one half plain. Mix the coffee dissolved in water into the other. Divide cake mixtures in half again and pour onto the prepared trays. Bake for 8–12 minutes or until the tops of each cake spring back when lightly touched. Carefully remove the baking parchment and allow cakes to cool.

Spread the reserved butter and sugar mixture in between each layer of the cake, alternating coffee and plain.

Press down gently to even the layers. Cover the sides with the butter and sugar mixture. Press the flaked almonds into the sides and dust the top with icing sugar.

**STEP ONE:** *Spread the coffee flavoured cake layer with a quarter of the reserved buttercream mixture.*

**STEP TWO:** *Continue layering the cake slices with the buttercream.*

**STEP THREE:** *When all layers are joined, cover the sides with extra buttercream. Decorate with almonds and dust the top with icing sugar.*

# FLORENTINE TORTE

$A$*nyone who loves Florentine biscuits will adore this delicious combination of cake and Florentine topping.*

**2 quantities praline, hot (see page 158)**
**1 chocolate génoise sponge (see page 59)**
**1 quantity quick no-fuss chocolate buttercream (see page 156)**
**roasted flaked almonds (see page 171)**

Line a baking tray (sheet) with baking parchment. Grease the ring of a 23 cm (9 in) spring form pan and place on the tray. Pour the hot praline into the ring and spread evenly to the edges. Allow to cool slightly and remove the ring. While still warm, cut into 12 equal wedges with a hot, oiled, sharp knife. Cool.

### TO ASSEMBLE

Cut the sponge into quarters horizontally. Spread the first layer with chocolate buttercream and place next layer on top. Repeat until all layers have been used. Cover the top and sides with buttercream and press almonds around the sides of the cake. Decorate the top with praline wedges.

Chill for one hour before serving.

**STEP ONE:** *Pour the Florentine topping into a greased cake ring and spread to the edges of the ring.*

**STEP TWO:** *While still warm, cut the Florentine topping using a hot, oiled knife.*

**STEP THREE:** *When cold arrange the Florentine topping portions on the top of the finished cake.*

# PRINCESS CAKE

This Danish cake includes many of the features Scandinavians love in their desserts — sponge cake, cream, custard and marzipan.

### FILLING
250 ml (9 fl oz) cream (single or light)
250 ml (9 fl oz) milk
250 g (9 oz) sugar
50 ml (1 ³/₄ fl oz) cream (single or light), extra
50 ml (1 ³/₄ fl oz) milk, extra
75 g (2 ¹/₂ oz) custard powder
2 x 60 g (2 oz, large) eggs
4 drops yellow food colouring

1 vanilla génoise sponge (see page 58)
200 ml (7 fl oz) crème Chantilly (see page 164)

### TO DECORATE
500 g (17 ¹/₂ oz) marzipan, tinted green (see page 169)
100 g (3 ¹/₂ oz) marzipan, tinted yellow (see page 169)
dark (plain or semi-sweet) chocolate, melted
(see page 159)

Line the sides and base of a 23 cm (9 in) spring form pan with baking parchment.

Place the cream, milk and sugar in a saucepan and bring to the boil over a low heat. Blend together the extra cream, extra milk, custard powder, eggs and food colouring and add to the heated cream mixture. Cook over a low heat until the mixture boils and thickens, stirring constantly. Divide filling in half. Chill one half.

### TO ASSEMBLE
Cut the sponge in half horizontally. Place one layer in the prepared pan and spoon on the unchilled filling. Top with the second layer of sponge. Chill the cake for 40 minutes. When the filling is completely cold, remove the rim of the pan.

Gently fold crème Chantilly into the chilled filling to make a smooth, stiff cream. Cover the sides of the cake with the cream and place a mound of cream on the top in the centre. Shape the mound to form a smooth dome. Chill for 15 minutes. Roll out the green marzipan thinly and drape it over the chilled cake, moulding to fit. Drizzle melted chocolate over the top. Decorate with small yellow marzipan flowers and green marzipan leaves.

STEP ONE: *Remove the chilled custard-filled cake from the pan and cover the top and sides with crème Chantilly to form a dome in the centre of the cake.*

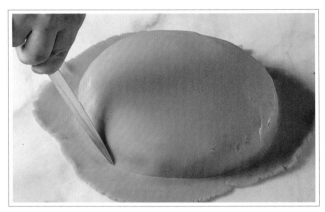

STEP TWO: *Roll out the green marzipan thinly until it covers the entire domed cake. Mould the marzipan over the cake and crème so that an even, smooth surface is achieved.*

STEP THREE: *Place the melted chocolate into a piping (pastry) bag and drizzle the chocolate over the top of the marzipan covering. Decorate with yellow marzipan flowers.*

# Spiral Sponge Torte

*This torte may look complicated, but if you can make a Swiss Roll you can make a Spiral Sponge Torte.*

### Base
*105 g (3 ³/₄ oz) plain (all-purpose) flour*
*50 g (1 ³/₄ oz) icing (powdered) sugar*
*70 g (2 ¹/₂ oz) unsalted butter, cut into small pieces*
*1 x 60 g (2 oz, large) egg, lightly beaten*

### Sponge
*90 g (3 oz) plain (all-purpose) flour*
*50 g (1 ³/₄ oz) cocoa powder*
*8 x 60 g (2 oz, large) eggs*
*200 g (7 oz) caster (superfine) sugar*

*200 g (7 oz) strawberry jam*
*1 quantity French buttercream (see page 156)*
*30 ml (1 fl oz) Grand Marnier*

### To Decorate
*chocolate curls (see page 162)*
*icing (powdered) sugar*
*125 g (4 ¹/₂ oz) flaked almonds, roasted (see page 171)*

### Base
Place the flour, icing sugar and butter in a bowl and very lightly rub in the butter until the mixture resembles coarse breadcrumbs. Add the egg and mix to a firm dough. Wrap the dough in plastic (cling) wrap and chill for one hour.

Preheat oven to 180 deg C (350 deg F). Grease a 23 cm (9 in) flat round tray lightly with butter. Roll the chilled dough into a 23 cm (9 in) circle and place on the prepared baking tray. Bake for 8–10 minutes or until golden brown. Cool in the pan on a wire rack.

### Sponge
Line four 28 cm x 20 cm (11 in x 8 in) baking trays (sheets) with baking parchment. Sift the flour and cocoa twice.

Beat the eggs and sugar until thick and fluffy and the mixture forms a ribbon (see page 172). Very gently fold in by hand the sifted flour and cocoa. Pour the mixture into the prepared trays and bake for 10–12 minutes or until the sponges have shrunk slightly away from the sides of the trays and the top springs back when lightly touched. Cool on the trays.

### To Assemble
Cover the pastry base with a thin layer of strawberry jam. Cut the sponges into 6 cm (2 ³/₈ in) strips and coat each strip with a thin layer of jam and buttercream. Roll one strip into a spiral and place in the centre of the pastry base. Remove the spring form cake rim. Continue to wrap strips of sponge around the first spiral until the pastry base is covered. Very carefully replace the rim of the pan around the torte. Close the rim in position and chill for one hour.

Sprinkle torte with Grand Marnier and cover the top with buttercream. Remove the rim, spread the sides with buttercream and press with flaked almonds. Decorate the top with chocolate curls and dust with icing sugar.

**Step One:** *Cover the pastry base with jam and cut each sponge into strips the same height as the cake pan.*

**Step Two:** *Cover the strips evenly with jam and buttercream. Roll the sponge strip carefully toward yourself, taking care not to split the sponge.*

**STEP THREE:** *Place the spiral in the centre of the pastry base.*

**STEP FOUR:** *Remove the spring form cake rim, and beginning where the first spiral ended, coil the next sponge strip around the first.*

**STEP FIVE:** *When the pastry base is covered, carefully replace the cake rim. Chill for one hour.*

**STEP SIX:** *Sprinkle with Grand Marnier and cover the top of the cake with buttercream.*

**STEP SEVEN:** *Carefully remove the rim from the sides of the cake by running a knife around the top of the ring. Spread buttercream around the side of the cake and cover with roasted flaked almonds.*

**STEP EIGHT:** *Decorate with chocolate curls. Place paper strips across the torte and dust with icing sugar. Carefully remove the paper.*

# ZUG CHERRY TORTE

This *Kirsch-flavoured cake is named after the historic Swiss town of Zug.*

SYRUP
*200 g (7 oz) caster (superfine) sugar*
*100 ml (3 1/2 fl oz) water*
*180 ml (6 1/4 fl oz) Kirsch*

*1 vanilla génoise sponge (see page 58)*
*2 japonaise bases (see page 57)*
*1 quantity Italian buttercream (see page 157)*
*12 maraschino cherries for decorating*

Place the sugar and water in a saucepan and bring to the boil. Cook slowly for 15 minutes. Remove from the heat and add the Kirsch. Chill for one hour.

Cut the sponge horizontally 3 cm (1 1/4 in) from the top and 3 cm (1 1/4 in) from the bottom. Discard the top and bottom layers. Pour the cooled syrup on the remaining middle layer.

Place a japonaise base on a serving dish and spread thinly with a little of the buttercream. Top with the soaked sponge and spread with buttercream. Top with the remaining japonaise base. Press lightly to spread the filling and cover the top and sides of the cake with the remaining buttercream. Decorate the top with cherries.

# PRINCE REGENT TORTE

*There have been many Prince Regents waiting to become King. Eating this torte is surely a regal way to pass the time.*

*1 quantity japonaise base, uncooked (see page 57)*
*1 quantity Dobos Torte filling (see page 1)*
*250 g (9 oz) marzipan (see page 168)*

### TO DECORATE
*400 g (14 oz) dark (plain or semi-sweet) chocolate, melted (see page 159)*
*whole hazelnuts*

Preheat oven to 180 deg C (350 deg F). Line six baking trays (sheets) with baking parchment and draw 23 cm (9 in) circles on each.

Spread the japonaise mixture into the circles on the prepared trays and bake for 15–20 minutes. Cool on baking parchment on a wire rack.

### TO ASSEMBLE
Cover each japonaise base with Dobos Torte filling and stack one on top of the other. Cover the top and sides of the torte with the filling. Roll out the marzipan thinly and cover the whole torte. Spread melted chocolate smoothly and evenly over the marzipan. When the chocolate is set, cut the torte into wedges with a hot, sharp knife and decorate each wedge with whole hazelnuts.

**STEP ONE:** *Layer each of the japonaise bases alternately with the filling. Cover the top and sides of the cake with the same mixture.*

**STEP TWO:** *Cover the entire cake with a thin layer of marzipan.*

**STEP THREE:** *Pour the melted chocolate over the marzipan and spread to achieve a smooth, even coating.*

# VENICE CITRUS TORTE

T*he chocolate gondolas floating on the top of this torte may take a little practice to get just right but they add a really distinctive touch to the chocolate and citrus flavours.*

*1 chocolate génoise sponge (see page 59)*
*1 japonaise base made from $^1/_2$ quantity (see page 57)*
*$^1/_2$ quantity orange flavoured buttercream (see page 156)*
*$^1/_2$ quantity lemon flavoured buttercream (see page 157)*
*60 g (2 oz) maraschino cherries, drained and chopped*
*300 g (10 $^1/_2$ oz) marzipan, tinted pink (see page 169)*
*chocolate gondolas (see page 163)*

Cut the sponge into quarters horizontally. Cover the meringue base with a thin layer of orange buttercream and cover with maraschino cherries. Top with a layer of sponge and spread with lemon buttercream. Place a second layer of sponge on top and spread with orange. Repeat, alternating buttercream until all the layers of sponge are used. Spread the top and sides of the cake with a thin layer of orange buttercream. Roll out the marzipan thinly and wrap around the side of the cake to make a marzipan collar. Lightly mark 12 even wedges on the top of the cake and decorate each portion with orange buttercream rosettes. Decorate with the chocolate gondolas.

**STEP ONE:** *Cover the japonaise base with buttercream and chopped cherries. Layer each slice of sponge alternately with the two buttercreams.*

**STEP TWO:** *When all the layers have been joined together, cover the top and sides of the cake with buttercream.*

**STEP THREE:** *Cover the sides of the cake with the marzipan collar and lightly mark 12 wedges on the torte. Pipe buttercream rosettes on each portion.*

# TRUFFLE TORTE

*T*here are some cakes that true chocoholics
remember forever. This rich, creamy, milk chocolate
Truffle Torte is one of them.

FILLING
*160 ml (5 ¹/₂ fl oz) milk*
*160 ml (5 ¹/₂ fl oz) cream (single or light)*
*530 g (18 ¹/₂ oz) milk chocolate, chopped*
*300 g (10 ¹/₂ oz) unsalted butter*
*550 g (19 ¹/₂ oz) caster (superfine) sugar*
*220 ml (7 ³/₄ fl oz) water*
*8 egg whites*
*130 g (4 ¹/₂ oz) caster (superfine) sugar, extra*

BASE
*2 japonaise bases ( see page 57)*

*cocoa powder for dusting*

Place the milk and cream in a saucepan and bring to
the boil. Remove from the heat, add the chocolate
and stir until melted. Cool, but do not refrigerate.
When set, cream with the butter until the mixture is
light and has increased in volume.

Place the sugar and water in a saucepan, bring to
the boil and heat to 120 deg C (250 deg F). Test
temperature with a sugar (candy) thermometer.

Beat the egg whites until stiff peaks form (see
page 173). Add the sugar. When the sugar syrup
reaches the correct temperature, pour slowly onto
the beaten egg whites, beating all the time until the
filling is cool. Mix a small amount of the filling into
the cooled mixture. Very gently fold in by hand the
remaining meringue.

Spread three quarters of the filling onto one of
the bases and top with the other base. Press gently on
the top to spread the filling evenly. Spread the
remaining filling on the top, reserving sufficient to
pipe TRUFFLE across the top of the torte. Chill for 2
hours before serving. Dust with cocoa powder.

# PANAMA CAKE

PAT
B-DAY
07

**A** *beautiful tasting, fine-textured cake. If you like nutty flavours then this is the cake for you.*

### CAKE
*6 egg yolks*
*1 x 60 g (2 oz, large) egg*
*90 g (3 oz) icing (powdered) sugar*
*50 g (1 ³/₄ oz) ground hazelnuts*
*5 egg whites*
*50 g (1 ³/₄ oz) sponge cake, crumbed*
*60 g (2 oz) ground almonds*
*40 g (1 ¹/₂ oz) plain (all-purpose) flour*

### TO DECORATE
*1 quantity quick no-fuss chocolate buttercream (see page 156)*
*100 g (3 ¹/₂ oz) flaked almonds, roasted (see page 171)*
*cocoa powder*

Preheat oven to 180 deg C (350 deg F). Grease a 23 cm (9 in) spring form pan lightly with butter and line the base with baking parchment.

Beat the egg yolks, egg and sugar until light and fluffy and the mixture forms a ribbon (see page 172). Mix in the ground hazelnuts. Beat the egg whites until stiff peaks form (see page 173). Mix a large spoonful of the beaten egg whites into the beaten yolks by hand. Very gently fold in the remainder of the egg whites, the cake crumbs, almonds and flour.

Pour into the prepared pan and bake for 35–45 minutes or until the cake has shrunk slightly away from the sides of the pan and the top springs back when lightly touched. Cool in the pan for 5 minutes before turning out onto a wire rack.

When completely cold, cut the cake into thirds horizontally. Spread two layers with buttercream and stack one on top of the other. Top with the remaining layer and cover the top and sides with the remaining buttercream. Press flaked almonds onto the top and sides. Dust with cocoa powder.

# MONT BLANC

A *very rich cake with a japonaise base and core of berries enveloped by crème Chantilly and chestnut purée. Like Mont Blanc — not for the faint-hearted.*

*¹/₂ (cut horizontally) chocolate génoise sponge (see page 59)*
*400 g (14 oz) canned sweetened chestnut purée*
*600 ml (21 fl oz) crème Chantilly (see page 164)*
*1 japonaise base (see page 57)*
*8 maraschino cherries*
*fresh berries of the season*

Cut a 10 cm (4 in) circle out of the centre of one layer of sponge and discard. Spread a small amount of crème Chantilly on top of the japonaise base. Top with the sponge ring. Using most of the remaining crème Chantilly, pile it on top of the ring shaping it to form a mound around the well in the centre.

Mix the chestnut purée until smooth and creamy. Fill a piping bag (pastry bag) fitted with a star nozzle with purée and pipe up the sides and over the mound to the centre. Repeat until the cake is covered. Fill a piping bag fitted with a star nozzle with the crème Chantilly and pipe rosettes around the top edge. Decorate rosettes with maraschino cherries and fill the well with fresh berries. Chill.

**STEP ONE:** *With the sponge ring on top of the japonaise base, cover with crème Chantilly shaping it to form a mound.*

**STEP TWO:** *Pipe the softened chestnut purée over the crème Chantilly mound.*

**STEP THREE:** *Decorate the top edge with crème Chantilly rosettes and cherries. Fill the centre with berries.*

# PUNCH TORTE

*P*unch *Torte takes its name from the punch-like syrup used to soak the slices of génoise sponge.*

### BASE
*100 g (3 ¹/₂ oz) plain (all-purpose) flour*
*45 g (1 ¹/₂ oz) icing (powdered) sugar*
*60 g (2 oz) unsalted butter, softened*
*1 x 60 g (2 oz, large) egg*
*2 teaspoons water*

### SYRUP
*150 ml (5 ¹/₄ fl oz) dark rum*
*2 cinnamon sticks*
*200 g (7 oz) caster (superfine) sugar*
*50 ml (1 ³/₄ fl oz) water*
*100 ml (3 ¹/₂ fl oz) orange juice*
*60 g (2 oz) apricot jam*

*1 vanilla génoise sponge (see page 58)*
*150 g (5 ¹/₄ oz) apricot jam, extra*

### TO DECORATE
*apricot glaze (see page 166)*
*225 g (8 oz) marzipan*
*150 g (5 ¹/₄ oz) white chocolate*
*60 g (2 oz) dark (plain or semi-sweet) chocolate, melted (see page 159)*
*200 g (7 oz) flaked almonds, roasted (see page 171)*

Place the flour and icing sugar in a bowl and very lightly rub in the butter until the mixture resembles coarse breadcrumbs. Add the egg and sufficient water to make a firm dough. Wrap the dough in plastic (cling) wrap and chill for one hour.

Preheat oven to 180 deg C (350 deg F). Grease the base of a 23 cm (9 in) spring form pan lightly with butter and roll out the chilled dough to fit the prepared base. Bake for 5–10 minutes or until the top is a light golden brown. Cool.

### SYRUP
Place the rum, cinnamon sticks, sugar, water, orange juice and apricot jam in a saucepan and bring to the boil. Cook for 10 minutes. Cool and strain.

### TO ASSEMBLE
Spread the cooled pastry base with warm apricot jam. Cut the sponge into quarters horizontally. Stack each layer of sponge on top of the pastry base, spreading each layer with cooled syrup and jam. Coat the top and sides with warm apricot glaze.

On a lightly floured bench, roll out the marzipan into a 23 cm (9 in) circle. Pour white chocolate over the marzipan. Pipe dark chocolate on top of the white chocolate. Use the feathering technique (see page 168) to decorate. When set use a hot, sharp knife to cut the marzipan and chocolate circle into 12 wedges. Place on top of the cake and press flaked almonds around the sides.

**STEP ONE:** *Brush each of the four layers with syrup and jam. Stack each sponge layer on top of the pastry base. Coat the top and sides of the cake with apricot glaze.*

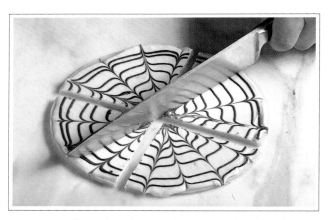

**STEP TWO:** *Use a hot, sharp knife to cut the firm chocolate and marzipan top into 12 portions. Place on the surface of the cake.*

# BÛCHE DE NOËL

This cake is a Christmas favourite in many countries and is known by as many names: Snow Log, Yule Log, Chocolate Log and Christmas Tree Cake. The French version is called Bûche De Noël.

*1 vanilla génoise sponge, uncooked (see page 58)*
*caster (superfine) sugar*

To Decorate
*1 quantity quick no-fuss chocolate buttercream (see page 156)*
*225g (8 oz) marzipan*
*dark (plain or semi-sweet) chocolate, melted, for piping (see page 160)*
*marzipan holly and berries (see page 171)*

Preheat oven to 180 deg C (350 deg F). Grease a 20 cm x 30 cm (8 in x 12 in) baking tray (sheet) lightly with butter and line with baking parchment. Spread a tea towel on a bench (counter) and cover with greaseproof (waxed) paper. Sprinkle the paper with caster sugar.

Pour the uncooked génoise sponge mixture onto the prepared tray and bake for 15–18 minutes or until the top of the sponge springs back when lightly touched.

Turn out onto the greaseproof paper and remove the baking parchment. Trim the crusty edges of the sponge with a knife. Cover the sponge with another sheet of greaseproof paper and position with a long side nearest you. Grasp the furthest ends of the tea towel and carefully roll the sponge around the top sheet of paper. Allow to cool. When cold, unroll and remove the paper and spread the sponge with half the buttercream. Roll up the sponge again and refrigerate for 30 minutes.

Cut a 5 cm (2 in) slice off the end of the log with a sharp knife and, using a little buttercream, attach to the log to resemble a broken branch. Roll the marzipan thinly. Cut 3 discs the same diameter as the log. With the melted chocolate, pipe growth rings onto each disc and leave to dry. Using a little buttercream, attach discs to both ends of the log and the broken branch.

Pipe the remaining buttercream onto the log, using a star nozzle to make the bark texture. Decorate with marzipan holly and berries.

**STEP ONE:** *Place the chocolate-decorated marzipan discs on the ends of the log.*

**STEP TWO:** *Using a star nozzle, pipe bark texture onto the cake, piping only in one direction.*

**STEP THREE:** *When the cake is covered with buttercream decorate with marzipan holly and berries.*

# MEN'S TORTE

When this alcoholic torte was first made in Germany men were thought to be the only ones who could eat it. Popular nowadays in the coffee houses of Germany, it should be renamed Everybody's Torte.

*1 chocolate génoise sponge (see page 59)*

FILLING
*600 ml (21 fl oz) dry white wine*
*180 g (6 1/4 oz) sugar*
*80 g (2 3/4 oz) custard powder*
*120 ml (4 1/4 fl oz) water*
*3 x 60 g (2 oz, large) eggs, lightly beaten*

TO DECORATE
*250 g (9 oz) marzipan*
*200 g (7 oz) dark (plain or semi-sweet) chocolate, melted (see page 159)*
*100 g (3 1/2 oz) flaked almonds, roasted (see page 171)*
*12 maraschino cherries*

Line the base and sides of a 23 cm (9 in) spring form pan with baking parchment. Slice the sponge into quarters horizontally and place the top layer into the prepared pan.

Place the wine and sugar in a saucepan and bring to the boil. Blend the custard powder and water and stir into the lightly beaten eggs. Pour in the hot wine syrup, beating all the time. Return the mixture to the saucepan and heat, stirring all the time until the custard boils and thickens.

Pour a third of the custard into the prepared pan and top with a layer of sponge. Repeat with the custard and layers of sponge. Press down lightly to spread the filling evenly and chill for 2 hours.

Roll the marzipan into a 23 cm (9 in) circle and cover with chocolate. With a hot knife cut the circle into 12 wedges.

Cut the chilled cake into 12 wedges and top each with a marzipan wedge. Support each wedge with a maraschino cherry and tilt as pictured.

Press flaked almonds around the side of the torte.

# CHOCOLATE TRUFFLE CAKE

This cake has layers of chocolate génoise sponge separated by very rich creamy chocolate filling. Pure indulgence.

*1 chocolate génoise sponge (see page 59)*

### FILLING
*200 g (7 oz) unsalted butter, softened*
*200 g (7 oz) dark (plain or semi-sweet) chocolate, melted (see page 159)*
*60 g (2 oz) caster (superfine) sugar*
*650 ml (23 fl oz) cream (single or light), at room temperature*
*150 g (5 ¼ oz) hazelnuts, chopped*
*cocoa powder for dusting*

Beat the butter until creamy and fluffy. Gradually add the chocolate and mix well, scraping down the insides of the bowl to ensure that no lumps form. Beat in the sugar. Slowly add the cream by drizzling it down the sides of the bowl. If the mixture is too cold it may curdle and separate. To remedy this, warm a quarter of the mixture over low heat and beat into the remaining mixture. Fold in the hazelnuts. If the mixture is very runny, chill until firm and then beat.

### TO ASSEMBLE
Slice the sponge into quarters horizontally. Place the first layer on a serving plate and spread with one fifth of the filling. Place the next layer of sponge on top. Repeat with the remaining filling and sponge layers, reserving about two fifths of the filling to cover the top and sides. Dust with cocoa powder and chill.

# SWISS ROLL

*Rolled sponges are very easy to make. Have everything ready to roll before the cake is cooked and be prepared to work very quickly when the cake is turned out onto the sugared paper.*

*80 g (2 ³/₄ oz) plain (all-purpose) flour*
*80 g (2 ³/₄ oz) cornflour (cornstarch)*
*caster (superfine) sugar*
*100 g (3 ¹/₂ oz) marzipan, softened*
*10 egg yolks*
*10 egg whites*
*200 g (7 oz) caster (superfine) sugar, extra*
*250 g (9 oz) strawberry jam, warmed*
*icing (powdered) sugar for dusting*

**STEP ONE:** *When the jam has been spread over the sponge, trim the edges of the sponge with a knife and carefully roll the sponge, in the paper, toward yourself.*

Preheat oven to 200 deg C (400 deg F). Grease a 23 cm x 20 cm x 1 cm (9 in x 8 in x ¹/₂ in) Swiss Roll pan very lightly with butter and line with baking parchment. Sift the flours twice. Sprinkle a large sheet of greaseproof paper with caster sugar.

Crumble the marzipan into the egg yolks in a mixing bowl and beat until the mixture is stiff, white and foamy. Beat the egg whites until stiff peaks form (see page 173) and gradually add the extra sugar a spoonful at a time. Beat until the sugar is dissolved. Take a spoonful of the egg white mixture and mix by hand into the marzipan mixture. Very gently fold in the sifted flours and the remainder of the egg whites. Pour into the prepared pan and bake for 20–25 minutes or until the top of the sponge springs back when lightly touched and the sponge has shrunk slightly away from the sides of the pan. Turn the sponge out onto the sugared greaseproof paper and trim the crusty edges. It is important to work quickly. Spread the sponge with jam. Then with a short side nearest you, start rolling the sponge tightly toward you. Place the roll, seam side down, on the greaseproof paper and roll the greaseproof paper over the Swiss Roll. Using a scraper, further tighten the roll. Dust with icing sugar and serve in thin slices.

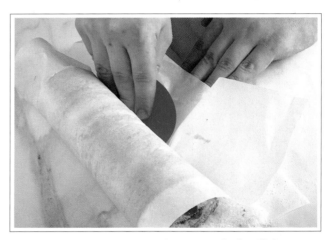

**STEP TWO:** *When the sponge sheet is completely rolled, use a plastic scraper to tighten the rolls, pressing inwards between the top and bottom sheets of paper.*

# Gâteau Fraisier

When you are making this gâteau, position the strawberries around the outside edge of the crème to form an attractive pattern.

*1 vanilla génoise sponge (see page 58), baked in a 20 cm (8 in) square pan*
*1 quantity crème Chantilly (see page 164)*
*500 g (17 ½ oz) small strawberries, hulled and halved*
*200 g (7 oz) apricot glaze (see page 166)*
*250 g (9 oz) marzipan, tinted green (see page 169)*

### To Decorate
*royal icing in a piping (pastry) bag (see page 167)*
*dark (plain or semi-sweet) chocolate, melted for piping (see page 160)*

Trim the crusty edges of the sponge and cut in half horizontally. Spread the bottom layer with all the crème Chantilly. Press strawberries into the sides of the crème layer. Place the second layer of sponge on top of the crème Chantilly and coat with warm apricot glaze. Roll out the marzipan into a 20 cm (8 in) square and place on top of the cake. For extra effect, texture the marzipan with a patterned rolling pin.

Decorate the gâteau with piped royal icing (see page 167) and melted chocolate.

**Step One:** *Place the strawberries around the edge of the cake and fill the centre with the cream.*

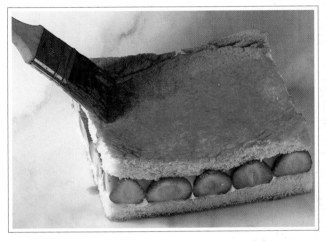

**Step Two:** *Place the top layer of sponge on top of the strawberries and coat with apricot glaze.*

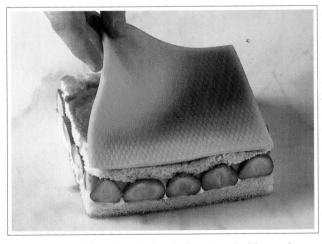

**Step Three:** *Place the thinly rolled and marked layer of green marzipan over the apricot glaze.*

# LE SUCCESS

$T$*his dessert is for those who love cake and meringue equally. Ground almonds are folded into beaten egg whites and sugar to make, when baked, a cake-like meringue.*

**5 egg whites**
**220 g (7 ³/₄ oz) caster (superfine) sugar**
**110 g (4 oz) ground almonds**
**40 g (1 ¹/₂ oz) cornflour (cornstarch)**
**40 g ( 1 ¹/₂ oz) icing (powdered) sugar**

### FILLING
**1 quantity quick no-fuss chocolate buttercream (see page 156)**

### TOPPING
**400 g (14 oz) chopped hazelnuts, for decoration**

Preheat oven to 180 deg C (350 deg F). Line four baking trays (sheets) with baking parchment and draw a 23 cm (9 in) circle on each.

Beat the egg whites until stiff peaks form (see page 173) and gradually add the sugar a spoonful at a time. Beat until the sugar is dissolved. Fold in by hand the ground almonds, cornflour and icing sugar. Place a quarter of the mixture in the centre of each circle and spread out evenly to the edges. Bake for 30 minutes. Cool on the trays on a wire rack.

When completely cold, spread buttercream thinly on each layer of cake and stack one on top of the other. Coat the top and sides smoothly with the remaining buttercream. Chill for 40 minutes. Press hazelnuts onto the top and sides. Chill for an hour before serving.

**STEP ONE:** *Join the layers together with thinly spread buttercream.*

**STEP TWO:** *Cover the top and sides of the cake with buttercream.*

**STEP THREE:** *Coat the cake with chopped hazelnuts.*

# MERINGUE GÂTEAU

Constantly check the meringue during browning as it takes only seconds for it to burn.

*1 buttercake (see page 101), baked in a 23 cm (9 in)
round cake pan
250 g (9 oz) apricot jam
15 canned apricot halves, drained
5 egg whites
150 g (5 ¼ oz) caster (superfine) sugar*

### TO DECORATE
*12 maraschino cherries, halved
150 g (5 ¼ oz) icing (powdered) sugar*

Preheat oven to 180 deg C (350 deg F). Cut the cake into quarters horizontally. Spread jam on each layer and stack one on top of the other. Cover the top with apricot halves.

Beat the egg whites in a mixing bowl until stiff peaks form (see page 173), then add the sugar a spoonful at a time. Beat until the sugar is dissolved. Cover the top and sides of the cake thickly with the meringue. Smooth. Place halved maraschino cherries around the edge of the cake and sprinkle with icing sugar. Bake for 5–10 minutes to set and brown the meringue.

**STEP ONE:** *After joining the layers of sponge together, place the drained apricots on the top of the cake.*

**STEP TWO:** *Cover the top and sides of the cake with the meringue mixture.*

**STEP THREE:** *Decorate the cake with cherries and dust lightly with icing sugar before browning in the oven.*

# HUMMINGBIRD CAKE

No one is sure who named this cake, but it is most appropriate as the cake is made with the fruit hummingbirds love.

*250 g (9 oz) plain (all-purpose) flour*
*250 g (9 oz) caster (superfine) sugar*
*1 level teaspoon salt*
*2 level teaspoons ground cinnamon*
*2 level teaspoons baking powder*
*2 x 60 g (2 oz, large) eggs*
*100 g (3 1/2 oz) canned crushed pineapple, drained*
*2 over-ripe bananas, peeled and mashed*
*60 ml (2 fl oz) pineapple juice*
*150 ml (5 1/4 fl oz) light (safflower) oil*

FILLING
*cream cheese frosting (see page 166)*

Preheat oven to 180 deg C (350 deg F). Grease a 23 cm (9 in) round deep cake pan lightly with butter and line base with baking parchment.

Place all the dry ingredients in a mixing bowl and mix thoroughly. Add the eggs, pineapple, bananas, pineapple juice and oil and mix thoroughly. Pour the mixture into the prepared pan and bake for 35–40 minutes or until a skewer inserted into the centre of the cake comes out dry and the cake has shrunk slightly away from the sides of the pan. Let stand for 10 minutes before turning out onto a wire rack to cool. When cold, cut the cake into halves horizontally and spread one third of the cream cheese frosting on top of the bottom layer. Top with the second layer and cover the top and sides of the cake with the remaining frosting.

# JAPONAISE

Japonaise is one of the great traditional recipes of the pâtissier's repertoire.

### MERINGUE BASE
**4 egg whites**
**150 g (5 1/4 oz) caster (superfine) sugar**
**100 g (3 1/2 oz) roasted almonds, ground**
**40 g (1 1/2 oz) cornflour (cornstarch)**
**20 g (3 2/3 oz) icing (powdered) sugar**

### TO DECORATE
**250 g (9 oz) quick no-fuss buttercream (see page 156)**
**200 g (7 oz) flaked almonds, roasted (see page 171)**
**icing (powdered) sugar for dusting**

Preheat oven to 180 deg C (350 deg F). Line two baking trays (sheets) with baking parchment and draw a 23 cm (9 in) circle on each.

Beat the egg whites until stiff peaks form (see page 173) and gradually beat in the sugar a spoonful at a time. Beat at top speed on the mixer for 15 minutes until the sugar is dissolved.

Mix the almonds, cornflour and icing sugar, then very gently fold in the beaten egg whites by hand.

Divide the mixture in half and carefully spoon into the marked circles, keeping the meringue within the edges.

Bake for 45–50 minutes. Cool on the trays on a wire rack. When the meringues are cold, spread one with buttercream and top with the second meringue.

Cover the top and sides with buttercream. Press flaked almonds on the top and sides. Dust lightly with icing sugar and chill for one hour before serving.

# GÉNOISE SPONGE
## (VANILLA)

A *Génoise Sponge is a truly unique French creation and is at the heart of many other cakes. By following this easy recipe and with a little practice you'll soon be making the perfect génoise.*

*140 g (5 oz) plain (all-purpose) flour*
*8 x 60 g (2 oz, large) eggs*
*140 g (5 oz) caster (superfine) sugar*
*25 g (³/₄ oz), unsalted butter, melted*
*1 teaspoon vanilla essence (extract)*

Preheat oven to 180 deg C (350 deg F). Sift the flour three times. Grease a 23 cm (9 in) spring form pan lightly with butter. Dust with a little plain flour and shake the pan to remove any excess.

Place the eggs, sugar and vanilla essence in the mixing bowl of an electric mixer and beat on the highest setting for 10–12 minutes or until the ribbon stage is reached (see page 172). Lightly sprinkle half of the sifted flour over the mixture and very gently fold in by hand. Repeat with the remaining flour and fold in the melted butter. Pour the mixture into the prepared pan and bake for 15–20 minutes or until the sponge has shrunk slightly away from the sides of the pan and the top springs back when lightly touched. Cool in the pan for 5 minutes before turning out onto a wire rack.

**STEP ONE:** *Beat the sugar and eggs until light and fluffy and the ribbon stage is achieved.*

**STEP TWO:** *Add the sieved flour to the egg mixture and slowly and carefully fold through the mixture. Be careful not to beat out too much air.*

**STEP THREE:** *After folding in the melted butter, pour the sponge mixture into a lightly greased and floured 23 cm (9 in) spring form cake pan.*

# GÉNOISE SPONGE

## (CHOCOLATE)

P A T
B-DAY
07

*The addition of a little cocoa powder transforms a Génoise Sponge 'ordinaire' into a Génoise Sponge 'extraordinaire'.*

*120 g (4 ¹/₄ oz) plain (all-purpose) flour*
*30 g (1 oz) cocoa powder*
*8 x 60 g (2 oz, large) eggs*
*140 g (5 oz) caster (superfine) sugar*
*30 g (1 oz) unsalted butter, melted*

Preheat oven to 180 deg C (350 deg F). Sift the flour and cocoa powder together three times. Grease a 23 cm (9 in) spring form pan lightly with butter. Dust with a little plain flour and shake the pan to remove any excess.

Place the eggs and sugar in the mixing bowl of an electric mixer and beat on the highest setting for 10–12 minutes or until the mixture forms a ribbon (see page 172). Lightly sprinkle half the sifted flour and cocoa over the mixture and very gently fold in by hand. Repeat with the remaining flour and cocoa and fold in the melted butter. Pour the mixture into the prepared pan and bake for 15–20 minutes or until the sponge has shrunk slightly away from the sides of the pan and the top springs back when lightly touched. Cool in the pan for 5 minutes before turning out onto a wire rack.

# CLASSIC FARE

## Elegant and traditional cakes

## HUNGARIAN CHOCOLATE TORTE

*This wonderful chocolate torte shows why Hungarians are so famous for their cooking.*

*5 egg yolks*
*100 g (3 1/2 oz) caster (superfine) sugar*
*400 g (14 oz) dark couverture chocolate, melted (see page 159)*
*200 g (7 oz) ground almonds*
*150 g (5 1/4 oz) plain (all-purpose) flour*
*100 ml (3 1/2 fl oz) brandy*
*5 egg whites*
*50 g (1 3/4 oz) caster (superfine) sugar, extra*

TO DECORATE
*apricot glaze (see page 166)*
*250 g (9 oz) marzipan (see page 168)*
*dark (plain or semi-sweet) chocolate, melted (see page 160) for chocolate collar*
*chocolate curls (see page 162)*

Preheat oven to 180 deg C (350 deg F). Grease a 23 cm (9 in) spring form pan lightly with butter and line the base with baking parchment.

Beat the egg yolks and sugar until thick and almost white and the mixture forms a ribbon (see page 172). Very gently fold in by hand the chocolate, almonds and brandy. Beat the egg whites until soft peaks form (see page 173), then beat in the extra sugar a spoonful at a time. Beat until the sugar is

dissolved. Very gently fold in by hand the beaten egg yolks and flour. Pour into the prepared pan and bake for 30–40 minutes or until the top of the cake springs back when lightly touched. Cool in the pan on a wire rack.

When completely cold, turn the cake out and cover the top and sides with the apricot glaze. Roll out the marzipan into a circle large enough to cover the top and sides of the cake. Place the marzipan over the cake and mould to fit neatly. Trim excess marzipan and make the chocolate collar (see steps 3, 4 and 5). Chill the torte until the chocolate collar is firm. Remove the baking parchment from the collar before decorating the top with chocolate curls.

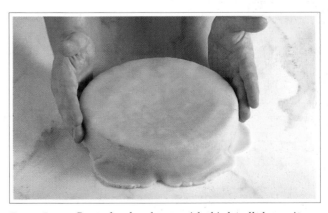

STEP ONE: *Cover the glazed torte with thinly rolled marzipan.*

**STEP TWO:** *Mould the marzipan around the top and sides of the cake and trim any excess from the base.*

**STEP THREE:** *Spread melted chocolate onto a strip of parchment approximately 1 cm (¹/2 in) higher than the cake is deep.*

**STEP FOUR:** *Wrap the chocolate collar around the sides of the marzipan-covered cake.*

**STEP FIVE:** *Make sure that the collar fits evenly and chill until the chocolate sets. When firm, carefully remove the parchment paper.*

**STEP SIX:** *Cover the inside of the cake with the smallest chocolate curls.*

**STEP SEVEN:** *Cover the top of the cake with the largest and neatest chocolate curls.*

# LEMON TORTE

*The lemons give the rich filling in this torte a delightful sharpness. It's a good finale for a late spring outdoor lunch or a summer barbecue.*

### BASE
*165 g (5 ³/₄ oz) plain (all-purpose) flour*
*85 g (3 oz) icing (powdered) sugar*
*105 g (3 ³/₄ oz) unsalted butter, cut into small pieces*
*1 x 60 g (2 oz, large) egg, lightly beaten*

### FILLING
**rind and juice of 5 medium-sized lemons**
**11 x 60 g (2 oz, large) eggs**
*480 g (17 oz) caster (superfine) sugar*
*380 ml (13 ³/₂ fl oz) cream (single or light)*
*apricot glaze (see page 166)*

### TO DECORATE
*200 g (7 oz) fondant, melted (see page 166)*
*flaked almonds, roasted (see page 171)*

Grease a 23 cm (9 in) spring form pan lightly with butter. Line the base with baking parchment.

Place the flour, icing sugar and butter in a bowl and very lightly rub in the butter until the mixture resembles coarse breadcrumbs. Add the egg and mix to make a firm dough. Wrap in plastic (cling) wrap and chill for one hour.

Preheat oven to 170 deg C (340 deg F). Roll out the chilled dough into a 27 cm (10 ¹/₂ in) circle and line the base and sides of the prepared pan.

Beat the lemon rind and juice, eggs, sugar and cream until thoroughly mixed and pour into the pan. Bake for 35–40 minutes or until golden brown and firm to the touch. Cool in the pan on a wire rack.

When cold, remove from pan and brush the top with apricot glaze and allow to dry before applying the melted fondant. Allow to dry. Sprinkle the top with almonds.

# DUAL TORTE

*The flavour and colour of chocolate and almond blend beautifully in this two-toned torte.*

**90 g (3 oz) flaked almonds**

### CHOCOLATE TORTE
**3 egg whites**
**60 g (2 oz) caster (superfine) sugar**
**90 g (3 oz) icing (powdered) sugar**
**115 g (4 oz) ground almonds**
**30 g (1 oz) cocoa powder**

### WHITE TORTE
**90 g (3 oz) plain (all-purpose) flour**
**1/8 level teaspoon baking powder**
**115 g (4 oz) butter**
**130 g (4 1/2 oz) caster (superfine) sugar**
**130 g (4 1/2 oz) ground almonds**
**2 x 60 g (2 oz, large) eggs**
**1 egg yolk**

Preheat oven to 180 deg C (350 deg F). Grease a 20 cm x 10 cm x 5 cm (8 in x 4 in x 2 in) bar pan generously with butter. Line the base with flaked almonds.

### CHOCOLATE TORTE
Beat the egg whites until stiff peaks form (see page 173), then beat in the caster sugar a spoonful at a time. Beat until the sugar is dissolved. Fold in the icing sugar, almonds and cocoa powder. Spread the mixture over the flaked almonds in the pan and up the sides as well.

### WHITE TORTE
Sift the flour and baking powder. Beat the butter, sugar and almonds until creamy, light and fluffy. Add the eggs, one at a time, then the egg yolk, beating very well after each one is added. Gently fold in by hand the sifted flour. Pour into the centre of the prepared pan.

Bake for 35–40 minutes or until the top of the cake springs back when lightly touched. Cool in the pan for 5 minutes before turning the torte out onto a wire rack.

**STEP ONE:** *Grease the bar pan and line the base with flaked almonds.*

**STEP TWO:** *Spread the chocolate mixture over the bottom and around the sides of the pan.*

**STEP THREE:** *Pour the white cake mixture in the centre of the chocolate mixture and spread evenly. Bake.*

# ORANGE SUPREME TORTE

*M*ade *without flour, this torte uses the entire orange — not just the zest and juice — to give it a rich and full-bodied flavour.*

*3 whole oranges*
*6 egg yolks*
*180 g (6 ¹/₂ oz) sugar*
*8 egg whites*
*1 level teaspoon baking powder*
*280 g (10 oz) ground almonds*

TO DECORATE
*apricot glaze (see page 166)*
*modelling chocolate (see page 163)*
*cocoa powder for dusting*

Preheat oven to 180 deg C (350 deg F). Grease a 23 cm (9 in) spring form pan lightly with butter and line base with baking parchment.

Place the oranges in a saucepan, cover them with water and bring to the boil. Boil the oranges for 1 ¹/₂ hours. Remove the oranges from the water while still hot and place them in a food processor or blender and blend them to a pulp.

Beat the egg yolks with 90 g (3 oz) of the sugar until it forms a ribbon (see page 172). Beat the egg whites until stiff peaks form (see page 173). Gradually beat in remaining sugar a spoonful at a time. Beat until the sugar is dissolved. Add the ground almonds and baking powder slowly to the meringue and beat the mixture until it is well combined.

Fold the egg yolk mixture into the orange pulp and then fold in the egg whites. Pour into the prepared pan. Bake for 30–40 minutes or until the cake has shrunk slightly away from the sides of the pan and the top of the cake springs back when lightly touched. Cool in the pan on a wire rack.

When it is completely cold, turn out and coat with warmed apricot glaze. To decorate the torte cover it with modelling chocolate and lightly dust the top with cocoa powder.

**STEP ONE:** *After coating the cake with warm apricot glaze, roll out the modelling chocolate approximately 3 mm (¹/₈ in) thick and wide enough to cover the cake easily.*

**STEP TWO:** *Stretch the modelling chocolate until it is wider than the cake and place it onto the glazed surface, allowing it to fall where and how it pleases.*

**STEP THREE:** *When the cake is completely covered with the chocolate, carefully mould the surface by hand to make folds in the chocolate, being careful not to flatten the top. Neaten the bottom edge of the chocolate.*

# DUTCH CRUMBLE TORTE

A *deliciously rich buttery cake with a pastry base topped with apricots, almonds and sultanas, and crowned with a crunchy cinnamon-flavoured topping.*

### BASE
*190 g (6 ¹/₂ oz) plain (all-purpose) flour*
*100 g (3 ¹/₂ oz) icing (powdered) sugar*
*140 g (5 oz) unsalted butter, cut into small pieces*
*1 x 60 g (2 oz, large) egg, beaten*
*15 ml (¹/₂ fl oz) water*

*apricot glaze (see page 166)*
*¹/₂ vanilla génoise sponge (see page 58), cut in half horizontally, only one half required*

### FILLING
*500 g (17 ¹/₂ oz) canned apricot halves, drained*
*100 g (3 ¹/₂ oz) sugar*
*100 g (3 ¹/₂ oz) ground almonds*
*60 g (2 oz) sultanas (golden raisins)*

### TOPPING
*130 g ( 4 ¹/₂ oz) sugar*
*180 g (6 ¹/₄ oz) plain (all-purpose) flour*
*90 g (3 oz) ground almonds*
*2 level teaspoons ground cinnamon*
*130 g (4 ¹/₂ oz) unsalted butter*
*icing (powdered) sugar for dusting*

Preheat oven to 200 deg C (400 deg F). Grease a 23 cm (9 in) spring form pan lightly with butter and line the base with baking parchment.

### BASE
Place the flour and icing sugar in a bowl. Add the butter and very lightly rub into the flour and icing sugar until the mixture resembles fresh breadcrumbs. Add the egg and sufficient water to make a firm dough. Wrap in plastic (cling) wrap and chill for 30 minutes.

### FILLING
Combine all the filling ingredients.

### TOPPING
Place all the topping ingredients in a bowl and rub in butter until mixture resembles fresh breadcrumbs.

### TO ASSEMBLE
Roll the chilled pastry into a circle large enough to cover the base and sides of the prepared pan. Ease the pastry into place and trim the edges. Brush the base with apricot glaze and top with one layer of sponge. Spoon on the apricot filling and press down very firmly to compact. Sprinkle with crumble topping and place pan on a baking tray (sheet) for 35 minutes. Cool in the pan on a wire rack. When the torte is cold, dust with icing sugar.

# HOTEL SACHER WIEN

Das Hotel Sacher Wien – 1876 von Eduard Sacher, Sohn des Erfinders der Original Sacher-Torte, eröffnet, ist eine österreichische Institution. Hier finden Sie Tradition, Wiener Charme, Komfort und Luxus. Seit 1934 führt das Haus die Familie Gürtler, der es stets ein Anliegen ist, dessen Tradition zu pflegen. Die Geschichte der weltberühmten Original Sacher-Torte begann 1832, als sie vom 16-jährigen Kocheleven Franz Sacher am Hofe des Fürsten Metternich als Dessert kreiert wurde. Seit damals ist sie die wohl bekannteste Torte der Welt und das handgeschriebene Originalrezept ein streng gehütetes Geheimnis des Hauses.

Verpackt in kleine Holzkistchen wird die Original Sacher-Torte in alle Welt versandt. Bei der Herstellung wird auf jegliche chemische Konservierungsstoffe verzichtet. Überzeugen Sie sich selbst von ihrem einzigartigen Geschmack oder überraschen Sie Ihre Freunde und Geschäftspartner mit diesem exklusiven Geschenk. Am besten schmeckt die Original Sacher-Torte mit ungesüßtem Schlagobers. Fachgerecht teilt man die süße Köstlichkeit mit einem befeuchteten Sägemesser.

*The Hotel Sacher Wien – opened in 1876 by Eduard Sacher, son of the creator of the Original Sacher-Torte – is an Austrian institution. Here you find tradition, Viennese charm, comfort and luxury. The Gürtler family has been running the Hotel Sacher since 1934, always taking a personal interest in maintaining its traditions. The history of the world-famous Original Sacher-Torte began in 1832, when the 16-year old apprentice cook Franz Sacher created this dessert at the court of Prince Metternich. In the meantime, it has become the most famous torte in the world and the hand-written recipe is a "state secret" of the hotel.*

*Packed in an elegant wooden box, the Original Sacher-Torte is delivered worldwide and contains no chemical additives. Taste it yourself or delight your friends and business partners with this exclusive gift. It is at its best served with unsweetened whipped cream. It is easiest to slice with a serrated knife moistened with water.*

*Original Sacher*

SELECTION

EIN STÜCK VON WIEN...

A PIECE OF VIENNA...

# CHOCOLATE PECAN TORTE

*T he simple apricot glaze finish on this torte not only looks impressive but highlights the deep rich chocolate colour and the flavour of the pecan nuts.*

*100 g (3 ¹/₂ oz) plain (all-purpose) flour*
*130 g (4 ¹/₂ oz) unsalted butter*
*130 g (4 ¹/₂ oz) caster (superfine) sugar*
*6 egg yolks*
*175 g (6 ¹/₄ oz) dark (plain or semi-sweet) chocolate, melted (see page 159)*
*175 g (6 ¹/₄ oz) pecan nuts, halved*
*6 egg whites*
*100 g (3 ¹/₂ oz) caster (superfine) sugar, extra*

TO DECORATE
*apricot glaze (see page 166)*

Preheat oven to 180 deg C (350 deg F). Grease a 23 cm (9 in) spring form pan very lightly with butter and line base and sides with baking parchment. Sift the flour.

Beat the butter and sugar until creamy, light and fluffy. Add the egg yolks one at a time, beating very well after each one is added. Add the chocolate. Mix in by hand the sifted flour and pecan nuts. Beat the egg whites until stiff peaks form (see page 173) and gradually beat in the extra sugar a spoonful at a time. Beat until the sugar is dissolved. Take a spoonful of the beaten egg whites and mix into the chocolate mixture. Gently fold in by hand the remaining beaten egg whites.

Pour into the prepared pan. Bake for 45–50 minutes or until the top springs back when lightly touched. Cool in the pan. When cold turn the cake out and coat the top and sides with apricot glaze.

# DUNDEE CAKE

*Named after the town of Dundee in Scotland, this rich, light fruit cake is always decorated with blanched almonds. This cake can be cooked in advance as it keeps well for several weeks.*

380 g (13 ¹/₂ oz) plain (all-purpose) flour
4 level teaspoons baking powder
275 g (9 ¹/₂ oz) unsalted butter
275 g (9 ¹/₂ oz) soft light brown sugar
5 x 60 g (2 oz, large) eggs
6 teaspoons apricot jam
100 g (3 ¹/₂ oz) ground almonds
350 g (12 ¹/₄ oz) seedless dark raisins
250 g (9 oz) sultanas (golden raisins)
100 g (3 ¹/₂ oz) mixed (candied) peel
30 ml (1 fl oz) milk
250 g (9 oz) blanched almonds, for decoration

Preheat oven to 180 deg C (350 deg F). Grease a 23 cm (9 in) spring form pan lightly with butter and line the base and sides with baking parchment. Mix the flour and baking powder and sift twice.

Beat the butter and sugar until creamy, light and fluffy. Add the eggs one at a time, beating very well after each one is added. Beat in the apricot jam. Mix in by hand the sifted flour and baking powder alternately with the almonds and dried fruit. Pour mixture into the prepared pan and brush lightly with the milk. Arrange the almonds on top and press into the cake. Bake for 1 ¹/₂ hours or until a skewer inserted into the centre of the cake comes out dry. If the cake is browning too quickly and the mixture is not cooked, cover the top with brown paper or aluminium foil. Cool in the pan for 15 minutes before turning out onto a wire rack.

# HAZELNUT TORTE

*The perfect accompaniment for a cup of strong
coffee. When serving, cut only very thin slices as
this is quite a dry torte.*

### BASE
**210 g (7 1/2 oz) plain (all-purpose) flour
100 g (3 1/2 oz) icing (powdered) sugar
130 g (4 1/2 oz) unsalted butter, cut into small pieces
1 x 60 g (2 oz, large) egg, lightly beaten
20 ml (3/4 fl oz) water**

### FILLING
**200 g (7 oz) unsalted butter
140 g (5 oz) caster (superfine) sugar, extra
3 x 60 g (2 oz, large) eggs, extra
200 g (7 oz) plain (all-purpose) flour
210 g (7 1/2 oz) ground hazelnuts**

### TO DECORATE
**100 g (3 1/2 oz) apricot glaze (see page 166)
100 g (3 1/2 oz) fondant (see page 166)
flaked almonds, roasted (see page 171)**

### BASE
Preheat oven to 170 deg C (340 deg F). Grease a 23
cm (9 in) spring form pan lightly with butter and
line base with baking parchment. Sift the flour.

Place the flour and icing sugar in a bowl. Add the
butter and very lightly rub into the flour and icing
sugar until the mixture resembles fresh breadcrumbs. Add the egg and water to make a firm
dough. Knead very lightly. Wrap in plastic (cling)
wrap and chill for 30 minutes.

### FILLING
Beat the butter and sugar until creamy, light and
fluffy. Add the eggs one at a time, beating very well
after each one is added. Fold in the flour and
hazelnuts.

Roll out three quarters of the chilled pastry into a
circle and line the base and sides of the prepared
pan. Pour in the hazelnut filling. Roll out the
remaining pastry thinly and cut into one cm (1/2 in)
strips. Arrange the strips in a lattice pattern on top of
the hazelnut filling. Bake for 35–40 minutes or until
cooked. Cool in the pan on a wire rack. When cool,
brush with apricot glaze and allow to dry before
applying the melted fondant. Press flaked almonds
around the top edges.

# PINEAPPLE UPSIDE DOWN CAKE

Upside Down Cakes are an American adaptation of the classic French apple dish, Tarte Tatin, where a caramelized sugar base covered with slices of apple and topped with pastry is cooked then inverted to reveal the apple tart.

*250 g (9 oz) plain (all-purpose) flour*
*2 level teaspoons baking powder*
*6 canned pineapple rings*
*6 glacé (candied) cherries*
*90 g (3 oz) unsalted butter*
*150 g (5 ¼ oz) caster (superfine) sugar*
*2 x 60 g (2 oz, large) eggs*
*100 ml (3 ½ fl oz) milk*
*apricot glaze (see page 166)*
*200 g (7 oz) flaked almonds, roasted (see page 171)*

Preheat oven to 180 deg C (350 deg F). Grease a 23 cm (9 in) spring form pan lightly with butter and line the base with baking parchment. Sift the flour and baking powder. Place the pineapple rings in the prepared pan and decorate with the cherries.

Beat the butter and sugar until creamy, light and fluffy.

Add the eggs one at a time, beating very well after each one is added. Add the sifted flour, baking powder and milk and pour the mixture over the pineapple rings. Bake for 25–30 minutes or until a skewer inserted into the centre of the cake comes out dry and the cake has shrunk slightly away from the sides of the pan. Let stand for 5 minutes before turning out onto a serving platter. Brush with apricot glaze and decorate around the edge with flaked almonds.

# HIGH TEA CAKE

*There is nothing quite like an English high tea with toasted muffins, sandwiches made with fresh bread and butter, and a choice of two, if not three, cakes. This simple cake is at its very best within minutes of leaving the oven.*

300 g (10 ¹/₂ oz) plain (all-purpose) flour
2 ¹/₂ level teaspoons baking powder
100 g (3 ¹/₂ oz) unsalted butter
300 g (10 ¹/₂ oz) caster (superfine) sugar
2 x 60 g (2 oz, large) eggs
250 ml (9 fl oz) milk
60 g (2 oz) desiccated (flaked) coconut
60 g (2 oz) sugar
4 level teaspoons ground cinnamon
100 g (3 ¹/₂ oz) unsalted butter, extra

Preheat oven to 180 deg C (350 deg F). Grease a 23 cm (9 in) spring form pan lightly with butter and line base with baking parchment. Sift the flour and baking powder twice.

Beat the butter and sugar until creamy, light and fluffy. Add the eggs one at a time, beating very well after each one is added. Add the sifted flour and baking powder alternately with the milk. Do not over mix. Pour into the prepared pan and bake for 35–40 minutes or until a skewer inserted into the centre of the cake comes out dry. Cool in the pan for 5 minutes before turning out onto a wire rack.

Mix coconut, cinnamon and sugar. Spread the extra butter over the top of the cake and sprinkle on the coconut mixture. Serve immediately.

# SACHER TORTE

In the late 1800s, Viennese hotelier Franz Sacher claimed the distinction of creating the Sacher Torte for Prince Metternich. Rival pâtisserie, Demels, disagreed and insisted that the torte was its original recipe. After a bitter law suit the Hotel Sacher won exclusive rights to the name and to market the cake worldwide.

140 g (5 oz) plain (all-purpose) flour
40 g (1 ¹/₂ oz) cocoa powder
180 g (6 ¹/₄ oz) unsalted butter
100 g (3 ¹/₂ oz) caster (superfine) sugar
7 egg yolks
40 g (1 ¹/₂ oz) ground hazelnuts
7 egg whites
160 g (5 ¹/₂ oz) caster (superfine) sugar, extra

TO DECORATE
apricot glaze (see page 166)
250 g (9 oz) apricot jam
250 ml (9 fl oz) Sacher Torte glaze (see page 167)
dark (plain or semi-sweet) chocolate, melted, for piping
(see page 160)

STEP ONE: *Remove glaze from the heat and allow to cool before pouring evenly over the cooled cake.*

STEP TWO: *After pouring the chocolate glaze, make sure no air bubbles form on the surface of the cake. Allow the excess to run down the sides of the cake and drip through the wire rack. When cold remove from the rack and serve.*

Preheat oven to 180 deg C ( 350 deg F). Grease a 23 cm (9 in) spring form pan very lightly with butter and line base with baking parchment. Mix the flour and cocoa and sift twice.

Beat the butter and sugar until creamy, light and fluffy. Gradually add the egg yolks and beat well. Gently fold in by hand the sifted flour and cocoa and the hazelnuts. Beat the egg whites until stiff peaks form (see page 173) and gradually add the extra sugar a spoonful at a time. Beat until the sugar is dissolved. Take a quarter of the beaten egg white and gently mix by hand into the mixture. Very gently fold in the remaining egg whites. Pour the mixture into the prepared pan and bake for 35–40 minutes or until the top of the cake is firm and springs back when lightly touched.

Cool in the pan for 5 minutes before turning out onto a wire rack.

When cold cut into quarters horizontally. Spread apricot glaze on each layer and stack one on top of the other. Boil the apricot jam until thickened and spread evenly over the top and sides of the cake. Allow to cool then coat with slightly warm Sacher Torte glaze. Decorate with piped melted chocolate.

# SAND CAKE

U*nlike its name, this cake is not gritty but a delicious, moist combination of fruit and cake.*

### BASE

*210 g (7 ¹/₂ oz) plain (all-purpose) flour*
*100 g (3 ¹/₂ oz) icing (powdered) sugar*
*135 g (4 ³/₄ oz) unsalted butter, cut into small pieces*
*1 x 60 g (2 oz, large) egg, lightly beaten*
*30 ml (1 fl oz) water*

### CAKE

*175 g (6 ¹/₄ oz) plain (all-purpose) flour*
*145 g (5 oz) cornflour (cornstarch)*
*3 level teaspoons baking powder*
*250 g (9 oz) unsalted butter*
*250 g (9 oz) caster (superfine) sugar*
*4 x 60 g (2 oz, large) eggs*
*200 g (7 oz) sour black cherries, pitted*
*75 g (2 ¹/₂ oz) ground almonds*
*icing (powdered) sugar for dusting*

### BASE

Place the flour and icing sugar in a bowl. Add the butter and very lightly rub into the flour until the mixture resembles fresh breadcrumbs. Add the egg and sufficient water to make a firm dough. Knead very lightly and wrap in plastic (cling) wrap. Chill for one hour.

### SAND CAKE

Preheat oven to 160 deg C (320 deg F). Grease a 23 cm (9 in) spring form pan lightly with butter and line base with baking parchment. Mix the flours and baking powder and sift twice.

Beat the butter and sugar until creamy, light and fluffy. Add the eggs, one at a time, beating very well after each one is added. Mix in by hand the sifted flours and baking powder.

### TO ASSEMBLE

Roll out the chilled pastry into a 35 cm (14 in) circle. Gently ease the pastry into the pan. Cover the pastry with the cherries and ground almonds. Top with the cake mixture. Bake for 45–60 minutes or until a skewer inserted into the centre of the cake comes out dry. Cool in the pan on a wire rack. Lightly dust with icing sugar and serve warm.

# VIENNESE APPLE TORTE

Austrians pride themselves on knowing how to make good pastry and insist that the best pastry in the world is to be found in the coffee shops of Vienna.

200 g (7 oz) plain (all-purpose) flour
200 g (7 oz) cornflour (cornstarch)
2 level teaspoons baking powder
300 g (10 ¹/₂ oz) unsalted butter
300 g (10 ¹/₂ oz) caster (superfine) sugar
4 x 60 g (2 oz, large) eggs
100 ml (3 ¹/₂ fl oz) milk
3 medium-sized green cooking apples, peeled,
cored and very finely sliced
100 g (3 ¹/₂ oz) currants

TOPPING
100 g (3 ¹/₂ oz) caster (superfine) sugar
100 g (3 ¹/₂ oz) unsalted butter
150 g (5 ¹/₄ oz) plain (all-purpose) flour
60 g (2 oz) ground almonds
icing (powdered) sugar for dusting

Preheat oven to 160 deg C (320 deg F). Grease a 25 cm x 25 cm x 3 cm (10 in x 10 in x 1 in) baking tray (sheet) lightly with butter and line with baking parchment. Mix the flours and baking powder and sift twice.

Beat the butter and sugar until creamy, light and fluffy. Add the eggs one at a time, beating very well after each one is added. Add the sifted flours to the creamed mixture alternately with the milk. Spread the mixture into the prepared pan and top with the sliced apples. Scatter the currants on top.

Mix all the topping ingredients and spread over the apple. Bake for 30–40 minutes or until cooked. Cool on the tray on a wire rack. When cold dust with icing sugar and cut into thin slices.

# HOLLANDER TORTE

*This wonderful walnut torte can be served as soon as it has cooled a little.*

### BASE
*210 g (7 1/2 oz) plain (all-purpose) flour*
*100 g (3 1/2 oz) icing (powdered) sugar*
*135 g (4 3/4 oz) unsalted butter, cut into small pieces*
*1 x 60 g (2 oz, large) egg, lightly beaten*
*15 ml (1/2 fl oz) water*
*100 g (3 1/2 oz) walnut halves*

### FILLING
*200 g (7 oz) unsalted butter*
*150 g (5 1/4 oz) caster (superfine) sugar*
*3 x 60 g (2 oz, large) eggs*
*200 g (7 oz) plain (all-purpose) flour*
*200 g (7 oz) ground walnuts*
*200 g (7 oz) walnut halves, extra*

*strawberry glaze (see page 166)*
*crushed nuts for decoration*

Grease a 23 cm (9 in) spring form pan lightly with butter. Line the base with baking parchment.

### PASTRY BASE
Place the flour and icing sugar in a bowl and very lightly rub in the butter until the mixture resembles coarse breadcrumbs. Add the egg and sufficient water to make a firm dough. Wrap in plastic (cling) wrap and chill for one hour.

Preheat oven to 180 deg C (350 deg F). Roll out the chilled dough into a 27 cm (10 1/2 in) circle and line the base and sides of the prepared pan. Sprinkle pastry base with walnut halves.

### FILLING
Beat the butter and sugar until creamy, light and fluffy. Add the eggs one at a time, beating very well after each one is added. Mix in by hand the flour and ground walnuts. Pour into the prepared pan, decorate top with extra walnut halves and bake for 35–40 minutes or until the top springs back when lightly touched. Cool in the pan on a wire rack. Brush with strawberry glaze and press crushed nuts around the top edges.

# FRANGIPANE TORTE

*Italian immigrant Frangipani achieved
immortality in French pâtisserie circles with his
creation of crème Frangipane.*

### BASE
*280 g (10 oz) plain (all-purpose) flour
140 g (5 oz) icing (powdered) sugar
180 g (6 1/4 oz) unsalted butter, cut into small pieces
2 x 60 g (2 oz, large) eggs, lightly beaten*

### FILLING
*200 g (7 oz) unsalted butter, cut into small pieces
200 g (7 oz) caster (superfine) sugar
3 x 60 g (2 oz, large) eggs
1 egg yolk
60 g (2 oz) plain (all-purpose) flour
200 g (7 oz) ground almonds
200 g (7 oz) apricot jam*

### TO DECORATE
*apricot glaze (see page 166)
200 g (7 oz) fondant (see page 166)
flaked almonds, roasted (see page 171)*

Preheat oven to 180 deg C (350 deg F). Grease a 23
cm (9 in) spring form pan lightly with butter and line
the base with baking parchment.

Place the flour and icing sugar in a bowl. Add the
butter and very lightly rub into the flour and icing
sugar until the mixture resembles fresh breadcrumbs. Add the eggs and knead lightly to make a
firm dough. Wrap in plastic (cling) wrap and chill for
30 minutes.

### FILLING
Beat the butter and sugar until light and creamy.
Gradually beat in the eggs and egg yolk, then fold in
the flour and almonds.

### TO ASSEMBLE
Roll out the pastry into a 35 cm (14 in) circle. Gently
ease pastry into the base of the pan and up the sides.
Spread apricot jam over the base and spoon on the
filling. Trim the pastry so it is level with the top of the
frangipane filling. Bake for 45–50 minutes or until
cooked. Cool in the pan on a wire rack. When cold
brush the top of the torte with apricot glaze and
allow to dry. Brush melted fondant over the glaze,
press flaked almonds around the top edges and allow
to dry.

# BAUMKUCHEN

*B*efore ovens were used this cake was baked on a
stick over an open fire. As the stick was rotated
over the fire a thin cake batter was poured along
it, baking as the stick was turned. The result was
a cake that resembled the growth rings you see on a
felled tree. Hence its name Baumkuchen — tree cake.

*45 g (1 ¹/₂ oz) plain (all-purpose) flour*
*45 g (1 ¹/₂ oz) cornflour (cornstarch)*
*250 g (9 oz) unsalted butter*
*90 g (3 oz) caster (superfine) sugar*
*50 g (1 ³/₄ oz) marzipan, softened (see page 168)*
*8 egg yolks*
*8 egg whites*
*100 g (3 ¹/₂ oz) caster (superfine) sugar, extra*
*15 g (¹/₂ oz) ground almonds*

### To Decorate
*200 g (7 oz) quick no-fuss chocolate buttercream (see*
*page 156)*
*cocoa powder for dusting*

Preheat oven to 200 deg C (400 deg F). Line four 18
cm x 28 cm x 6 cm (7 in x 11 in x 2 ¹/₂ in) baking
trays (sheets) with baking parchment. Mix the flours
and sift twice.

Beat the butter, sugar and marzipan until
creamy, light and fluffy. Gradually add the egg yolks
and beat well. Beat the egg whites until stiff peaks
form (see page 173) and gradually beat in the extra
sugar a spoonful at a time. Beat until the sugar is
dissolved. Fold in by hand the sifted flours and
almonds, then the creamed butter and sugar. Beat
for 30 seconds to mix thoroughly.

Spread the mixture evenly into the four prepared
trays. Bake for 10–12 minutes or until the tops of the
cakes are slightly brown and spring back when lightly
touched. Do not overcook.

Cut four sheets of baking parchment larger than
the cakes and spread them out on a bench top
(countertop). Working very quickly, turn one cooked
cake at a time onto a sheet of baking parchment.
With one of the short edges of the cake facing you,
carefully roll the cake by turning over the first few
centimetres of parchment which will cause the cake
to curl. Keep rolling the cake tightly.

Turn out a second cake and where the first cake
ends start the second cake. Repeat with the other two
cakes.

Chill for one hour. Cover with buttercream and
dust with cocoa powder.

**STEP ONE:** *Remove the paper from the first cake and,*
*beginning with the end furthest from you, roll lengthways.*

**STEP TWO:** *Tightly roll the whole layer.*

**STEP THREE:** *Place the end of the second cake where the first*
*cake ends.*

**STEP FOUR:** *Continue rolling both cakes together.*

**STEP FIVE:** *As each cake ends, begin rolling the next cake until all the cakes have been used.*

# APPLE MERINGUE CAKE

This cake has an egg-rich butter cake base covered with a layer of finely sliced apples and topped with snowy white meringue. Serve it warm with crème Chantilly.

### BASE
300 g (10 ½ oz) plain (all-purpose) flour
2 ½ level teaspoons baking powder
250 g (9 oz) unsalted butter
250 g (9 oz) caster (superfine) sugar
5 egg yolks
vanilla essence (extract) to taste
2 medium-sized cooking apples, peeled, cored and very finely sliced

### TOPPING
5 egg whites
150 g (5 ¼ oz) caster (superfine) sugar

### TO SERVE
crème Chantilly (see page 164)

Preheat oven to 180 deg C (350 deg F). Grease a 23 cm (9 in) spring form pan very lightly with butter and line base with baking parchment. Sift the flour and baking powder.

Beat the butter and sugar until creamy, light and fluffy. Add the egg yolks one at a time, beating very well after each one is added. Beat in the vanilla essence. Mix in by hand the sifted flour and baking powder. Pour into the prepared pan and arrange the apples on top.

Beat the egg whites until stiff peaks form (see page 173) and gradually beat in the extra sugar a spoonful at a time. Beat until the sugar is dissolved. Pipe the meringue over the layer of apple. Bake for 45 minutes. Let stand for 5 minutes before removing the rim of the pan, leaving the cake on the base. Place on a wire rack to cool.

Serve with crème Chantilly.

# GERMAN POPPY SEED CAKE

*Poppy seeds give this cake its splendid flavour. If you cannot find ground poppy seeds, lightly roast whole seeds for a few minutes and pulverize them in a coffee grinder or use a mortar and pestle.*

### BASE
*100 g (3 ¹/₂ oz) plain (all-purpose) flour*
*50 g (1 ³/₄ oz) icing (powdered) sugar*
*65 g (2 ¹/₄ oz) unsalted butter, cut into small pieces*
*1 x 60 g (2 oz, large) egg*

### FILLING
*350 g (12 ¹/₄ oz) ground poppy seeds*
*200 g (7 oz) sponge cake crumbs*
*150 ml (5 ¹/₄ fl oz) milk*
*550 ml (19 ¹/₂ fl oz) milk, extra*
*70 g (2 ¹/₂ oz) custard powder*
*3 egg yolks*
*200 g (7 oz) sugar*
*100 g (3 ¹/₂ oz) sultanas (golden raisins)*

### TOPPING
*100 g (3 ¹/₂ oz) caster (superfine) sugar*
*200 g (7 oz) plain (all-purpose) flour*
*150 g (5 ¹/₄ oz) unsalted butter*
*icing (powdered) sugar for dusting*

### BASE
Place the flour and icing sugar in a bowl. Add the butter and lightly rub into the flour and icing sugar until the mixture resembles fresh breadcrumbs. Add the egg and mix thoroughly. Turn the dough onto a lightly floured bench top (countertop) and knead lightly to form a dough. Wrap in plastic (cling) wrap and chill for 30 minutes.

### FILLING
Mix the poppy seeds, sponge cake crumbs and milk in a bowl and soak for 15 minutes.

Blend a little of the extra milk with the custard powder and egg yolks and put to one side. Place the remaining milk and the sugar in a saucepan and bring to the boil. When the mixture boils, pour slowly onto the custard powder and egg yolk mixture, beating all the time. Return the mixture to the saucepan and cook until it thickens, stirring all the time. Remove from the heat and pour over the poppy seed mixture. Add the sultanas and mix thoroughly.

Place all the topping ingredients in a bowl and rub in the butter until the mixture resembles coarse breadcrumbs.

Preheat oven to 180 deg C (350 deg F). Grease a 23 cm (9 in) spring form pan lightly with butter and line the base with baking parchment. Roll out the pastry into a 23 cm (9 in) circle and place in the prepared pan. Pour in the poppy seed filling and sprinkle on the topping. Bake for 45 minutes. Dust thickly with icing sugar while still hot. Cool in the pan on a wire rack. When cold, dust again with more icing sugar.

# MARBLE CAKE

**M**any generations of children have wondered at the magic of this cake and the clever way the swirls of colour remain separate from each other.

*270 g (9 1/2 oz) plain (all-purpose) flour*
*2 level teaspoons baking powder*
*160 g (5 1/2 oz) unsalted butter*
*210 g (7 1/2 oz) caster (superfine) sugar*
*3 x 60 g (2 oz, large) eggs*
*250 ml (9 fl oz) milk*
*red (cochineal) food colouring*
*40 g ( 1 1/2 oz) cocoa powder blended with 2 tablespoons water to form a paste*
*1/2 quantity quick no-fuss buttercream (see page 156)*

Preheat oven to 180 deg C (350 deg F). Grease a 20 cm x 10 cm x 5 cm (8 in x 4 in x 2 in) loaf pan very lightly with butter and line base with baking parchment. Mix the flour and baking powder and sift twice.

Beat the butter and sugar until creamy, light and fluffy. Add the eggs one at a time, beating very well after each one is added. Gently fold in by hand the sifted flour and baking powder alternately with the milk. Divide mixture into 3 bowls. Add a few drops of red food colouring to one; mix the blended cocoa and water into another; and leave the remaining mixture plain. Place a spoonful of each mixture in turn into the prepared pan. Bake for 35–40 minutes or until a skewer inserted into the centre of the cake comes out dry and the cake has shrunk slightly away from the sides of the pan. Cool in the pan for 5 minutes before turning out onto a wire rack.

When cold cover the top with buttercream.

# QUICK FRUIT CAKE

*B*usy *cooks will love this fruit cake. It's a make-bake-cool-and-eat kind of cake.*

280 g (10 oz) plain (all-purpose) flour
2 ¹/₂ level teaspoons baking powder
2 level teaspoons ground cinnamon
1 level teaspoon ground cloves
250 g (9 oz) unsalted butter
250 g (9 oz) caster (superfine) sugar
4 x 60 g (2 oz, large) eggs
45 g (1 ¹/₂ oz) marmalade
100 g (3 ¹/₂ oz) sultanas (golden raisins)
60 g (2 oz) mixed (candied) peel
60 g (2 oz) seedless (dark) raisins
80 g (2 ³/₄ oz) walnuts, almonds, and hazelnuts,
roughly chopped
icing (powdered) sugar for dusting

Preheat oven to 180 deg C (350 deg F). Grease a loaf pan 23 cm x 10 cm x 10 cm (9 in x 4 in x 4 in) lightly with butter and line with baking parchment. Mix the flour, baking powder, cinnamon and cloves and sift twice.

Beat the butter and sugar until creamy, light and fluffy. Add the eggs one at a time, beating very well after each one is added. Beat in the marmalade. Dust the dried fruit and nuts with a little of the sifted flour mixture to stop them sinking to the bottom of the cake. Mix fruit and nuts with the remaining sifted flour. Add to the butter mixture. Spoon the mixture into the prepared pan and bake for 2 hours or until a skewer inserted in the centre of the cake comes out dry. Cool in the pan for 20 minutes before turning out onto a wire rack. Dust with icing sugar.

# BANANA CAKE

A *reliable homestyle favourite, the secret to a wonderfully moist and more fully flavoured cake lies in using fruit which is just over-ripe.*

*250 g (9 oz) plain (all-purpose) flour*
*2 level teaspoons baking powder*
*1 level teaspoon bicarbonate soda (baking soda)*
*150 g (5 ¼ oz) butter*
*150 g (5 ¼ oz) caster (superfine) sugar*
*2 x 60 g (2 oz, large) eggs*
*3 ripe bananas*
*80 g (2 ¾ oz) walnut pieces*

### TO DECORATE
*1 quantity of lemon cream cheese frosting*
*(see page 166)*
*marzipan bananas (see page 169)*

Preheat oven to 180 deg C (350 deg F). Grease a 23 cm (9 in) spring form pan with butter and dust very lightly with flour. Sift the flour, baking powder and bicarbonate of soda.

Beat the butter and sugar until creamy, light and fluffy. Add the eggs one at a time, beating very well after each one is added. Lightly mash the bananas and stir them into the egg mixture until just combined. Fold in by hand the flour and baking powder. Lastly fold in the walnuts. Spoon the cake mixture into the prepared pan. Bake for 35–40 minutes or until a skewer inserted into the centre of the cake comes out dry. Turn the cake out onto a wire rack and allow it to cool completely.

When the cake is quite cold, cover the top and sides with lemon cream cheese frosting and decorate with marzipan bananas.

# BATTENBERG

This *popular English cake with its chequerboard design came originally from Germany, home of the Battenberg family.*

500 g (17 ¹/₂ oz) plain (all-purpose) flour
4 level teaspoons baking powder
500 g (17 ¹/₂ oz) unsalted butter
500 g (17 ¹/₂ oz) caster (superfine) sugar
8 x 60 g (2 oz, large) eggs
1 teaspoon vanilla essence (extract)
2–3 drops red (cochineal) food colouring
250 g (9 oz) apricot jam

TO DECORATE
500 g (17 ¹/₂ oz) marzipan (see page 168)
marzipan flowers and leaves (see page 170)

Preheat oven to 180 deg C (350 deg F). Grease two 20 cm x 10 cm x 5 cm (8 in x 4 in x 2 in) bar pans lightly with butter and line with baking parchment. Mix the flour and baking powder and sift twice.

Beat the butter and sugar until creamy, light and fluffy. Add the eggs one at a time, beating very well after each one is added. Gently mix in by hand the sifted flour and baking powder. Add the vanilla essence. Do not over mix. Spoon half the mixture into one of the prepared pans and to the remaining half add the red colouring drop by drop until the mixture is the desired colour. Spoon into the second pan. Bake for 40–45 minutes or until a skewer inserted into the centre of the cakes comes out dry and the cakes have shrunk slightly away from the sides of the pans. Leave the cakes in the pans for 5 minutes before turning out onto a wire rack to cool.

When cold, cut each cake in half lengthways and then in half again. Brush each of the pieces with warmed apricot jam. Arrange the eight pieces to form a chequerboard pattern of alternating colours. Spread apricot jam on all four long sides of the cake. Roll out the marzipan into a rectangle long enough to wrap around the cake, a little wider than the cake and about 3 mm (¹/₈ in) thick. Cover the cake with marzipan. Crimp the top edges and decorate with marzipan flowers and leaves.

**STEP ONE:** *Cut each cake in half lengthways and then in half again.*

**STEP TWO:** *Brush each piece with warm apricot jam.*

**STEP THREE:** *Join the pieces together, alternating colours.*

**STEP FOUR:** *When all eight pieces of cake are joined together, brush apricot jam around the four sides.*

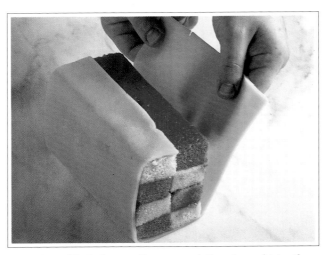

**STEP SIX:** *Wrap the marzipan around the cake and trim the edges.*

**STEP FIVE:** *Roll out the marzipan thinly and cut into a rectangle long enough to wrap around the cake and slightly wider.*

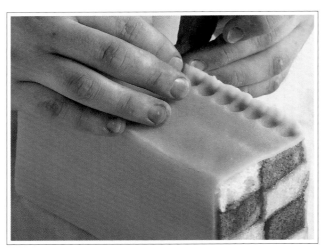

**STEP SEVEN:** *Pinch the top edge of the marzipan with your fingers for decoration.*

# MADEIRA CAKE

A *slice of Madeira Cake and a glass of Madeira was a traditional English refreshment to offer guests. People liked the contrast of the sharp citrus flavoured cake and the mellow warmth of the wine.*

345 g (12 ¹/₄ oz) plain (all-purpose) flour
3 level teaspoons baking powder
360 g (12 ¹/₂ oz) unsalted butter
360 g (12 ¹/₂ oz) caster (superfine) sugar
6 x 60 g (2 oz, large) eggs
125 g (4 ¹/₂ oz) ground almonds
grated rind and juice of 2 lemons
icing (powdered) sugar for dusting

Preheat oven to 170 deg C (340 deg F). Grease two 20 cm x 10 cm x 5 cm (8 in x 4 in x 2 in) loaf pans lightly with butter and line with baking parchment. Mix the flour and baking powder and sift twice.

Beat the butter and sugar until creamy, light and fluffy. Add the eggs one at a time, beating very well after each one is added. Gently fold in by hand the sifted flour and baking power, almonds and lemon juice and rind. Do not over mix. Pour into the prepared pans. Bake for 35–40 minutes or until a skewer inserted into the centre of each cake comes out dry and the cake has shrunk slightly away from the sides of the pan.

Cool for 5 minutes before turning out onto a wire rack.

When cold, dust with icing sugar.

# SIMNEL CAKE

The name of this traditional Easter cake comes from the Roman 'Siminellus' which was a bread eaten during spring fertility festivals.

300 g (10 ½ oz) plain (all-purpose) flour
2 ½ level teaspoons baking powder
2 level teaspoons ground cinnamon
2 level teaspoons mixed spice
270 g (9 ½ oz) unsalted butter
210 g (7 ½ oz) caster (superfine) sugar
5 x 60 g (2 oz, large) eggs
grated rind of one orange
60 ml (2 fl oz) orange juice
120 g (4 ¼ oz) ground almonds
150 g (5 ¼ oz) currants
150 g (5 ¼ oz) sultanas (golden raisins)
60 g (2 oz) seedless (dark) raisins
500 g (17 ½ oz) marzipan (see page 168)
dark (plain or semi-sweet) chocolate, melted
(see page 159)
marzipan, tinted (see page 169), for eggs

Preheat oven to 170 deg C (340 deg F). Grease a 23 cm (9 in) spring form pan very lightly with butter and line the sides and base with 3 layers of baking parchment, bringing the level of the paper 2 ½ cm (1 in) above the edge of the pan. Mix the flour, baking powder and spices and sift twice.

Beat the butter and sugar until creamy, light and fluffy. Add the eggs one at a time, beating very well after each one is added. Mix in by hand the sifted flour and spices, orange rind and juice, almonds and dried fruit. Spoon half of the mixture into the prepared pan.

Roll out half of the marzipan into a 22 cm (8 ½ in) circle. Place on top of the cake mixture in the pan. Spoon on the remaining cake mixture. Bake for 2 hours or until a skewer inserted into the centre of the cake comes out dry. Cool in the pan on a wire rack.

When cold remove from the pan and cover the top of the cake with a second circle of marzipan. Crimp the edges. Decorate with marzipan eggs and piped melted chocolate.

# BLUEBERRY TORTE

*The flavour of blueberries goes exceptionally well with the sour (soured) cream in this torte. But always use FRESH blueberries.*

*175 g (6 ¹/₄ oz) plain (all-purpose) flour*
*2 level teaspoons bicarbonate of soda (baking soda)*
*2 level teaspoons baking powder*
*175 g (6 ¹/₄ oz) unsalted butter*
*300 g (10 ¹/₂ oz) caster (superfine) sugar*
*3 x 60 g (2 oz, large) eggs*
*20 ml (³/₄ fl oz) lemon juice*
*350 g (12 ¹/₄ oz) blueberries*
*300 ml (10 ¹/₂ fl oz) sour (soured) cream*

### TO DECORATE
*1 quantity lemon cream cheese frosting (see page 166)*
*blueberries for garnish*

Preheat oven to 170 deg C (340 deg F). Grease a 23 cm (9 in) spring form pan lightly with butter and line the base with baking parchment. Mix the flour, bicarbonate of soda and baking powder and sift twice.

Beat the butter and sugar until creamy, light and fluffy. Add the eggs one at a time, beating very well after each one is added. Gently fold in by hand the sifted flour. Fold in the lemon juice, blueberries and sour cream. Pour into the prepared pan and bake for 1 ¹/₂ hours or until a skewer inserted into the centre of the cake comes out dry. Cool in the pan on a wire rack.

When cold, remove from the pan and cover the top and sides of the torte with frosting and decorate with blueberries.

# ANGEL FOOD CAKE

This version of America's favourite cake is truly the 'food of the angels'.

160 g (5 1/2 oz) plain (all-purpose) flour
30 g (1 oz) cornflour (cornstarch)
10 egg whites
1/4 level teaspoon cream of tartar
3 drops of lemon juice
300 g (10 1/2 oz) caster (superfine) sugar
3 teaspoons vanilla essence (extract)

To Decorate
1 quantity vanilla frosting (see page 165)

Preheat oven to 180 deg C (350 deg F). Grease a 23 cm (9 in) spring form pan very lightly with butter and dust with a little flour. Shake to remove excess. Sift the flours.

Beat the egg whites, cream of tartar and lemon juice until stiff peaks form (see page 173), then gradually beat in the sugar a spoonful at a time. Beat until the sugar is dissolved. Very gently fold in by hand the sifted flours and vanilla essence.

Pour the mixture into the prepared pan. Bake for 35–40 minutes or until the top springs back when lightly touched. Turn the pan upside down onto a wire rack and allow the cake to cool in the pan. When cold, turn out the cake and cover the top and sides with vanilla frosting.

# DEVIL'S FOOD CAKE

*This 'food for the devil' chocolate cake is sinfully rich.*

*350 g (12 ¹/₄ oz) plain (all-purpose) flour*
*2 ¹/₂ level teaspoons baking powder*
*4 level teaspoons bicarbonate of soda (baking soda)*
*60 g (2 oz) cocoa powder*
*125 g (4 ¹/₂ oz) unsalted butter*
*360 g (12 ¹/₂ oz) soft brown sugar*
*2 x 60 g (2 oz, large) eggs, lightly beaten*
*150 g (5 ¹/₄ oz) dark (plain or semi-sweet) chocolate, melted (see page 159)*
*230 ml (8 fl oz) milk*
*1 teaspoon vanilla essence (extract)*

### TO DECORATE
*1 quantity chocolate frosting (see page 166)*

Preheat oven to 180 deg C (350 deg F). Grease a 23 cm (9 in) spring form pan lightly with butter and line the base with baking parchment. Sift the flour, baking powder, bicarbonate of soda and cocoa powder twice.

Beat the butter and sugar until light and fluffy. Add the eggs, one at a time, beating well after each one is added. Add the chocolate. Mix in by hand the sifted flour alternately with the milk and vanilla essence. Pour into the prepared pan and bake for 35–40 minutes or until a skewer inserted into the centre comes out dry. Cool in the pan on a wire rack.

When cold cover the top and sides of the cake with chocolate frosting.

# PRALINE RING

*O̶ften the simplest dessert ideas are the very best. This German cake baked in a special ring pan is very easy to make and a snap to decorate. For a special occasion, fill the centre with fresh berries or rich handmade chocolates.*

375 g (13 ¼ oz) plain (all-purpose) flour
4 level teaspoons baking powder
250 g (9 oz) unsalted butter
250 g (9 oz) caster (superfine) sugar
4 x 60 (2 oz, large) eggs
30 ml (1 fl oz) milk
100 g (3 ½ oz) praline, crushed (see page 158)

### TO DECORATE
1 quantity quick no-fuss buttercream (see page 156)
400 g (14 oz) praline, crushed, extra

Preheat oven to 160 deg C (320 deg F). Grease a 23 cm (9 in) savarin pan (ring mold) lightly with butter and dust lightly with a little flour. Mix the flour and baking powder and sift twice.

Beat the butter and sugar until creamy, light and fluffy. Add the eggs one at a time, beating very well after each one is added. Mix in by hand the sifted flours and baking powder and fold in the milk and praline. Do not over mix. Pour into the prepared pan and bake for 35–40 minutes or until the cake has shrunk slightly away from the sides of the pan. Turn the cake out onto a wire rack to cool.

When the cake is quite cold, cover with butter-cream and lightly sprinkle with praline.

# ORANGE CAKE

Orange cake is an anytime favourite with children. Adults also like the flavour of this easy-to-make cake.

180 g (6 ¼ oz) plain (all-purpose) flour
2 level teaspoons baking powder
180 g (6 ¼ oz) unsalted butter
160 g (5 ½ oz) caster (superfine) sugar
grated rind and juice of 2 oranges
3 x 60 g (2 oz, large) eggs
60 g (2 oz) ground almonds

TO DECORATE
orange frosting (see page 165)
slices of fresh orange

Preheat oven to 180 deg C (350 deg F). Grease a 23 cm (9 in) spring form pan lightly with butter and line the base with baking parchment. Mix the flour and baking powder and sift twice.

Beat the butter and sugar until creamy, light and fluffy. Mix in the orange rind and juice and beat very well. Add the eggs one at a time, beating very well after each one is added. Mix in by hand the sifted flour and baking powder and the almonds. Do not over mix. Pour into the prepared pan and bake for 35–40 minutes or until a skewer inserted in the centre of the cake comes out dry and the cake has shrunk slightly away from the sides of the pan. Cool in the pan on a wire rack.

When cold, remove from the pan and cover the top of the cake with orange frosting.

Decorate with slices of fresh orange.

# ALKAZAR

This thin, rich almond cake topped with a lattice of marzipan is definitely one for connoisseurs of marzipan.

**8 egg yolks**
**160 g (5 ¹/₂ oz) caster (superfine) sugar**
**325 g (11 ¹/₂ oz) ground almonds**
**160 g (5 ¹/₂ oz) unsalted butter, melted and cooled**
**8 egg whites**
**160 g (5 ¹/₂ oz) caster (superfine) sugar, extra**

**TO DECORATE**
**225 g (8 oz) marzipan**
**150 g (5 ¹/₄ oz) caster (superfine) sugar**
**3 egg whites, lightly beaten**
**250 g (9 oz) strawberry jam**
**apricot glaze (see page 166)**
**125 g (4 ¹/₂ oz) flaked almonds, roasted**
**(see page 171)**

Preheat oven to 180 deg C (350 deg F). Grease a 23 cm (9 in) spring form pan with butter and line the base with baking parchment.

Beat egg yolks and sugar until thick and pale and the mixture forms a ribbon (see page 172). Gently fold in by hand the almonds and butter. Beat the egg whites until stiff peaks form (see page 173) and gradually beat in the extra sugar a spoonful at a time. Beat until the sugar is dissolved. Take a spoonful of the mixture and mix by hand into the beaten egg yolks. Gently fold in the remaining beaten egg whites. Pour the mixture into the prepared pan. Bake for 25–30 minutes or until the cake has shrunk slightly away from the sides of the pan and the top springs back when lightly touched. Cool on a wire rack for 15 minutes.

Preheat oven to 220 deg C (425 deg F). Blend the marzipan and sugar with sufficient egg white to make a soft paste that can be piped without losing its shape. Fill a piping (pastry) bag fitted with a plain ¹/₂ cm (¹/₄ in) nozzle with the marzipan mixture and pipe a lattice pattern on top of the cake. Pipe strawberry jam into the diamond-shaped spaces. Bake for 5 minutes or until the marzipan browns slightly and the jam forms a skin. Cool in the pan on a wire rack for 30 minutes. Remove cake from pan and chill.

When cold brush the sides with apricot glaze and press flaked almonds onto the glaze. Paint a little apricot glaze onto the marzipan lattice using a fine brush.

**STEP ONE:** *Pipe the marzipan in diagonal lines across the cold cake.*

**STEP TWO:** *Pipe strawberry jam into the diamond shaped holes.*

# Tiffany Cake

*This American fruit cake, as bright and glowing as a stained glass window, is fast becoming a favourite in place of the traditional fruit cake.*

*100 g (3 ¹/₂ oz) plain (all-purpose) flour*
*1 level teaspoon baking powder*
*90 g (3 oz) cocoa powder*
*70 g (2 ¹/₂ oz) glacé (candied) ginger*
*100 g (3 ¹/₂ oz) glacé (candied) pineapple*
*250 g (9 oz) glacé (candied) cherries*
*125 g (4 ¹/₂ oz) seedless (dark) raisins*
*250 g (9 oz) pitted dates*
*200 g (7 oz) mixed (candied) peel*
*180 g (6 ¹/₄ oz) walnut halves*
*200 g (7 oz) brazil nuts, whole*
*125 g (4 ¹/₂ oz) pecan halves*
*180 g (6 ¹/₄ oz) caster (superfine) sugar*
*4 x 60 g (2 oz, large) eggs, lightly beaten*
*6 egg yolks, lightly beaten*
*20 ml (³/₄ fl oz) vanilla essence (extract)*

Preheat oven to 130 deg C (260 deg F). Grease a 23 cm (9 in) spring form pan lightly with butter. Line the base and sides with two layers of baking parchment. Sift the flour, baking powder and cocoa powder.

Place the ginger, fruit and nuts into a bowl. Reserve two handfuls of the best whole fruit and nuts for the topping and set aside. Mix the sifted flour and sugar into the fruit and nuts then add the beaten eggs and vanilla essence. Spoon the mixture into the prepared pan and press the reserved fruit and nuts into the top. Bake for 2 hours or until a skewer inserted into the centre of the cake comes out dry. Cool in the pan on a wire rack.

# BUTTERCAKE

Good tasting buttercakes can be served plain for morning tea, sliced and dressed with whipped cream for high tea, or lightly toasted and topped with maple syrup for brunch or supper. This rich cake keeps well and is ideal for cake decorators who want to avoid the expense of using solid fruit cakes.

> 280 g (10 oz) plain (all-purpose) flour
> 1 level teaspoon baking powder
> 180 g (6 1/4 oz) unsalted butter
> 200 g (7 oz) caster (superfine) sugar
> 3 x 60 g (2 oz, large) eggs
> 250 ml (9 fl oz) milk
> icing (powdered) sugar, for dusting

Preheat oven to 180 deg C (350 deg F). Grease a 23 cm (9 in) spring form pan lightly with butter and line base with baking parchment. Sift the flour and baking powder.

Beat the butter and sugar until creamy, light and fluffy. Add the eggs one at a time, beating very well after each one is added. Mix in the sifted dry ingredients alternately with the milk. Pour the mixture into the prepared pan. Bake for 1–1 1/2 hours or until a skewer inserted in the centre of the cake comes out dry. Cool in the pan for 5 minutes then turn out onto a wire rack. When cold, dust with icing sugar.

# DEER'S BACK TORTE

It is easy to see why this traditional German cake is sometimes called the hedgehog.

250 g (9 oz) unsalted butter
115 g (4 oz) caster (superfine) sugar
60 g (2 oz) dark (plain or semi-sweet) chocolate, melted (see page 159)
9 egg yolks
300 g (10 1/2 oz) chocolate génoise sponge, crumbed (see page 59)
150 g (5 1/4 oz) ground almonds
60 g (2 oz) plain (all-purpose) flour
9 egg whites
115 g (4 oz) caster (superfine) sugar, extra
125 g (4 1/2 oz) flaked almonds
500 g (17 1/2 oz) dark (plain or semi-sweet) chocolate, melted

Preheat oven to 180 deg C (350 deg F). Grease a 30 cm (12 in) Balmoral pan with butter and dust lightly with flour. Beat the butter and sugar until creamy, light and fluffy. Beat in the chocolate. Add the egg yolks one at a time, beating well after each one is added. Fold in the cake crumbs, ground almonds and flour. Beat the egg whites until stiff peaks form (see page 173), then beat in the extra sugar a spoonful at a time. Beat until the sugar is dissolved. Take a spoonful of the beaten egg whites and mix into the creamed butter and sugar. Very gently fold in by hand the remaining egg whites.

Pour into the prepared pan and bake for 35–40 minutes or until a skewer inserted in the centre of the cake comes out dry. Cool cake in the pan for 5 minutes before turning out onto a wire rack.

Leave the cake on a wire rack and when cold cover the top and sides with protruding flaked almonds. Stand the wire rack on a metal tray and pour the extra melted chocolate thickly over the cake. Allow to set.

NOTE: *The chocolate that collects on the tray can be saved and used later.*

# PEAR CAKE

*This is the cake to make when beautiful Comice pears are in season.*

*500 g (17 ¹/₂ oz) ripe pears, peeled, cored and coarsely grated*
*480 g (17 oz) soft light brown sugar*
*180 g (6 ¹/₄ oz) walnuts, chopped*
*390 g (13 ¹/₂ oz) plain (all-purpose) flour*
*4 level teaspoons baking powder*
*2 level teaspoons ground cinnamon*
*230 ml (8 fl oz) light (safflower) oil*
*3 x 60 g (2 oz, large) eggs*

TO DECORATE
*1 quantity lemon cream cheese frosting (see page 166)*
*ground cinnamon*

Preheat oven to 180 deg C (350 deg F). Grease a 23 cm (9 in) spring form pan lightly with butter and line the base with baking parchment. Mix the pears, sugar and walnuts and let stand for 30 minutes. Mix the flour, baking powder and cinnamon and sift twice.

Mix the oil and eggs into the pear mixture and very gently mix in by hand the sifted flour. Pour into the prepared pan and bake for one hour or until a skewer inserted in the centre of the cake comes out dry. Cool in the pan on a wire rack.

When completely cold, remove from the pan and cover the top and sides with frosting. Dust the top lightly with cinnamon. Serve with slices of fresh pear.

# Toffee Cake

A *superb accompaniment to coffee, this cake can be served warm or cold. A dollop of cinnamon cream and this Toffee Cake becomes dessert.*

*180 g (6 ¼ oz) plain (all-purpose) flour*
*250 g (9 oz) unsalted butter*
*250 g (9 oz) caster (superfine) sugar*
*2 teaspoons vanilla essence (extract)*
*4 x 60 g (2 oz, large) eggs*
*125 g (4 ½ oz) dark (plain or semi-sweet) cooking*
*chocolate, melted and cooled (see page 159)*
*125 g (4 ½ oz) walnuts, chopped*
*3 level teaspoons cocoa powder mixed with 3 level*
*teaspoons icing (powdered) sugar for dusting*

Preheat oven to 200 deg C (400 deg F). Grease a 20 cm x 10 cm x 5 cm ( 8 in x 4 in x 2 in) bar pan lightly with butter and line with baking parchment. Sift the flour.

Beat the butter, sugar and vanilla essence together until creamy, light and fluffy. Add the eggs one at a time, beating very well after each one is added. Add the chocolate to the creamed butter and sugar mixture, mixing very quickly so that no lumps form. Mix the flour in by hand. Stir in the walnuts. Pour into the prepared pan and bake for 40 minutes or until a skewer inserted into the centre of the cake comes out dry. Cool in the pan on a wire rack.

Remove from pan to serve and dust with cocoa powder and icing sugar.

# CARROT CAKE

*Connoisseurs of the perfect Carrot Cake will like this recipe. It makes a cake that's moist, light and of just the right consistency.*

*50 g (1 ³/₄ oz) plain (all-purpose) flour*
*1 level teaspoon baking powder*
*7 egg yolks*
*175 g (6 ¹/₄ oz) caster (superfine) sugar*
*175 g (6 ¹/₄ oz) carrots, finely grated*
*90 g (3 oz) ground almonds*
*90 g (3 oz) ground hazelnuts*
*50 g (1 ³/₄ oz) dry breadcrumbs*
*7 egg whites*
*1 quantity lemon cream cheese frosting (see page 166)*
*100 g (3 ¹/₂ oz) flaked almonds, roasted (see page 171)*
*marzipan carrots (see page 169)*

Preheat oven to 180 deg C (350 deg F). Grease a 23 cm (9 in) spring form pan lightly with butter and line with baking parchment. Sift the flour and baking powder.

Beat the egg yolks and sugar until light, fluffy and almost white. Gently fold in by hand the carrots, almonds, hazelnuts, breadcrumbs and sifted flour and baking powder. Beat the egg whites until stiff peaks form (see page 173) and very gently fold into the beaten egg yolks. Pour into the prepared pan and bake for 30–35 minutes or until the cake has shrunk from the sides of the pan. Cool in the pan on a wire rack.

When the cake is completely cold, turn out onto a wire rack, cover the top and sides with frosting and press flaked almonds around the sides. Decorate with marzipan carrots and greenery such as parsley, dill or fennel for carrot leaves.

# OTHELLO

*This recipe uses an unusual technique. Flour, egg yolks and water are beaten for 30 minutes at top speed. After such a beating all the gluten strength in the flour has been destroyed, resulting in a very soft cake.*

*5 egg yolks*
*100 g (3 1/2 oz) plain (all-purpose) flour*
*160 ml (5 1/2 fl oz) water*
*5 egg whites*
*90 g (3 oz) caster (superfine) sugar*
*75 g (2 1/2 oz) cornflour (cornstarch)*
*250 g (9 oz) fondant, melted (see page 166)*
*60 g (2 oz) dark (plain or semi-sweet) chocolate, melted (see page 159)*

Place the egg yolks, flour and water in the bowl of an electric mixer and beat at top speed for 30 minutes.

Preheat oven to 160 deg C (320 deg F). Grease a 23 cm (9 in) spring form pan lightly with butter and line the base with baking parchment.

Beat the egg whites until stiff peaks form (see page 173) and beat in the sugar a spoonful at a time. Beat until the sugar is dissolved. Gently fold in by hand the cornflour. Take a spoonful of the egg whites and mix in by hand into the beaten egg yolks. Gently fold in the remaining egg whites. Pour the mixture into the prepared pan and bake for 40 minutes or until the top springs back when lightly touched. Cool in the pan for 5 minutes before turning out onto a wire rack.

When completely cold, heat the fondant until it is runny and smooth and mix in the melted chocolate. Pour three quarters of the melted fondant over the cake and allow to set. Place the remaining fondant in a piping (pastry) bag fitted with a writing nozzle and pipe the fondant on top of the cake to make a circular pattern.

**STEP ONE:** *Place the cake on a wire rack to cool and pour the chocolate fondant over the cake.*

**STEP TWO:** *Allow excess fondant to run down the sides of the cake and drain through the wire rack.*

**STEP THREE:** *Pipe a fondant circle from the centre of the cake to the edge.*

# Spice Gâteau

This light, spicy gâteau is topped with chocolate to make a perfect dessert or supper cake.

125 g (4 ¹/₂ oz) plain (all-purpose) flour
2 level teaspoons baking powder
1 level teaspoon ground cinnamon
1 level teaspoon ground ginger
150 g (5 ¹/₄ oz) sponge cake crumbs
125 ml (4 ¹/₂ fl oz) milk
100 g (3 ¹/₂ oz) unsalted butter
50 g (1 ¹/₂ oz) caster (superfine) sugar
4 level teaspoons honey
3 level teaspoons cocoa powder
2 x 60 g (2 oz, large) eggs

To Decorate
apricot glaze (see page 166)
250 g (9 oz) dark (plain or semi-sweet) chocolate,
melted (see page 159)

Preheat oven to 180 deg C (350 deg F). Grease a 23 cm (9 in) spring form pan very lightly with butter and line the base with baking parchment. Mix the flour, baking powder, cinnamon and ginger and sift twice. Soak the cake crumbs in milk. Beat the butter and sugar together until creamy, light and fluffy. Beat in the honey and cocoa. Add the eggs one at a time, beating very well after each one is added. Mix in by hand the sifted flour and spices. Stir in the soaked cake crumbs. Pour into the prepared pan and bake for 30–40 minutes or until a skewer inserted into the centre of the cake comes out dry. Cool the cake in the pan for 5 minutes before turning out onto a wire rack.

When the cake is cold cover the top and sides with apricot glaze. Allow to set and cool. Pour or spoon on the chocolate.

# ALMOND TORTE

This torte is moist and luscious with a crust of caramelized almonds. It is the perfect indulgence for those who like their sweets rich, heavy and slightly sinful to eat.

180 g (6 ¼ oz) ground almonds
60 g (2 oz) desiccated (flaked) coconut
250 g (9 oz) sugar
200 g (7 oz) unsalted butter, melted
4 x 60 g (2 oz, large) eggs, beaten

TO DECORATE
1 quantity praline, crushed (see page 158)
¼ quantity quick no-fuss buttercream (see page 156)

Preheat oven to 180 deg C (350 deg F). Grease a 23 cm (9 in) spring form pan lightly with butter. Dust with flour and shake out excess. Line the base with baking parchment.

Mix the almonds, coconut, sugar and butter together and blend in the beaten eggs. Pour the mixture into the prepared pan. Bake for 35–40 minutes or until cooled. Cool in the pan on a wire rack.

When cake is cold remove from the pan and spread buttercream evenly over the top. Sprinkle praline on the buttercream.

# LAS PALMAS

No one knows for certain why this cake should be named after Las Palmas in the Canary Islands, but the rich coconut flavours evoke images of a tropical paradise.

### CAKE
275 g (9 ¹/₂ oz) plain (all-purpose) flour
3 level teaspoons baking powder
3 x 60 g (2 oz, large) eggs
300 g (10 ¹/₂ oz) caster (superfine) sugar
125 ml (4 ¹/₂ fl oz) milk
50 g (1 ³/₄ oz) unsalted butter

### TOPPING
200 g (7 oz) unsalted butter
180 g (6 ¹/₄ oz) desiccated (flaked) coconut
300 g (10 ¹/₂ oz) soft light brown sugar
40 g (1 ¹/₂ oz) glucose (corn) syrup
160 ml (5 ¹/₂ fl oz) milk
vanilla essence (extract) to taste

200 g (7 oz) dark (plain or semi-sweet) chocolate, melted (see page 156)

Preheat oven to 180 deg C (350 deg F). Grease a 23 cm (9 in) spring form pan lightly with butter and line sides and base with baking parchment. Sift the flour and baking powder twice.

Beat the eggs and sugar until thick, light and fluffy and the mixture forms a ribbon (see page 172). Heat the milk and butter and gradually add to the beaten eggs beating all the time. The mixture will become thinner. Fold in by hand the sifted flour and baking powder and pour into the prepared pan. Bake for 35 minutes or until the top of the cake springs back when lightly touched and the cake has shrunk slightly away from the sides of the pan. Cool in the pan on a wire rack.

Place all the topping ingredients, except for the chocolate, in a saucepan and bring slowly to the boil. Cook slowly for 15 minutes and then pour over the cooling cake. Set oven temperature at 160 deg C (325 deg F), return cake to oven and bake for a further 15 minutes. Cool in the pan on a wire rack.

When completely cold remove from the pan. Turn base of cake uppermost and pour melted chocolate over the top. Spread the chocolate, allowing it to run down the sides of the cake. Chill. When the chocolate is set, turn the cake upright and place on a serving platter.

**STEP ONE:** *Turn the cold cake upside down on a wire rack and pour melted chocolate over the base.*

**STEP TWO:** *Spread the chocolate evenly and allow it to run down the sides of the cake. Leave to set.*

**STEP THREE:** *When the chocolate has set, turn the cake upright and serve.*

DAVID 60th B-DAY 2010 (smiley face)

# WALNUT TORTE

**M**any European cakes don't have any flour in them at all. Novice cooks often think the flour has been forgotten in the ingredients list but ground nuts are used instead.

300 *200 g (7 oz) dark chocolate, chopped*
9 *6 egg yolks*
150 *100 g (3 ¹/₂ oz) caster (superfine) sugar*
9 *6 egg whites*
150 *100 g (3 ¹/₂ oz) caster (superfine) sugar, extra*
300 *200 g (7 oz) ground walnuts*
*apricot glaze (see page 166)*
150 *100 g (3 ¹/₂ oz) ground walnuts, extra*
*100 g (3 ¹/₂ oz) walnut halves*
*icing (powdered) sugar*

Preheat oven to 180 deg C (350 deg F). Grease a 23 cm (9 in) spring form pan lightly with butter and line the base with baking parchment.

Place the chocolate in a bowl and melt over hot water. Beat the egg yolks and sugar until thick and pale and the mixture forms a ribbon (see page 172). Blend in the melted chocolate and ground walnuts quickly.

Beat the egg whites until stiff peaks form (see page 173) and gradually beat in the extra sugar a spoonful at a time. Beat until the sugar is dissolved. Take a spoonful of the mixture and mix by hand into the beaten egg yolks. Gently fold in the remaining beaten egg whites and extra ground walnuts.

Pour into the prepared pan and bake for 40–45 minutes. Place pan on a wire rack to cool before turning out. When cold cover the top and sides with apricot glaze. Decorate the top with the walnut halves. Dust heavily with icing sugar.

# CHRISTMAS CAKE

*Good cooks always make their Christmas cakes
months in advance as they know it takes time for
the rich flavours in the cake to fully mature.*

*100 g (3 1/2 oz) plain (all-purpose) flour*
*2 level teaspoons ground cinnamon*
*1 level teaspoon mixed spice (see page 172)*
*150 g (5 1/4 oz) unsalted butter*
*150 g (5 1/4 oz) light brown sugar*
*3 x 60 g (2 oz, large) eggs*
*60 ml (2 oz) golden syrup (light treacle)*
*250 g (9 oz) sultanas (golden raisins)*
*125 g (4 1/2 oz) seedless (dark) raisins*
*60 g (2 oz) mixed (candied) peel*
*60 g (2 oz) glacé (candied) cherries, red*
*60 g (2 oz) blanched almonds, chopped*

### TO DECORATE
*300 g (10 1/2 oz) marzipan (see page 168)*
*1 quantity of royal icing (see page 167)*
*marzipan holly and berries (see page 171)*

Grease a 23 cm (9 in) spring form pan lightly with
butter and line with 5 layers of greaseproof (waxed)
paper, bringing the level of the paper 2 1/2 cm (1 in)
above the rim of the pan. Preheat oven to 170 deg C
(340 deg F). Mix the flour, cinnamon and mixed
spice and sift twice.

Beat the butter and sugar until creamy, light and
fluffy. Add the eggs and golden syrup and beat well.
Mix the dried fruit and nuts alternately with the
sifted flour into the mixture. Spoon into the
prepared pan. Bake for 4 hours or until a skewer
inserted in the centre of the cake comes out dry.
Cool in the pan for 24 hours. Wrap the cake so that it
is airtight and store in a cool, dry place until
required.

### TO DECORATE
Remove greaseproof paper before decorating. Roll
out marzipan and cover the cake. Trim edges. With a
palette knife, spread royal icing over the top and
sides of the cake. Decorate with ribbon and marzipan
holly and berries.

# CHOCOLATE SOUFFLE GÂTEAU

*R*ich, sweet, yet light as a feather, this cake is meant to sink slightly in the centre and when cold is filled with light chocolate buttercream and decorated with neat chocolate squares.

*8 egg yolks*
*70 g (2 ¹/₂ oz) caster (superfine) sugar*
*250 g (9 oz) dark (plain or semi-sweet) chocolate, melted (see page 159)*
*110 g (4 oz) unsalted butter*
*10 g (¹/₃ oz) plain (all-purpose) flour*
*8 egg whites*

### TO DECORATE
*1 quantity chocolate French buttercream (see page 156)*
*16 chocolate squares (see page 161)*
*cocoa powder for dusting*

Preheat oven to 180 deg C (350 deg F). Grease a 23 cm (9 in) spring form pan lightly with butter and line the sides and base with baking parchment.

Beat the egg yolks and sugar until thick and almost white. Gently beat in by hand the melted chocolate and butter. Gently fold in the flour. Beat the egg whites until soft peaks form (see page 173) and gently fold into the egg yolk mixture. Pour the mixture into the prepared pan. Bake in the preheated oven for 35–40 minutes or until the gâteau has shrunk slightly away from the sides of the pan and the top springs back when lightly touched. Cool in the pan. The gâteau will sink in the middle as it cools.

When the gâteau is cold, cover the top and sides with chocolate French buttercream. Chill for one hour. Decorate the sides, then the top, with chocolate squares and dust with cocoa powder.

**STEP ONE:** *Cover the sides of the gâteau with the chocolate squares.*

**STEP TWO:** *Press any remaining squares or chocolate pieces onto the top of the gâteau. Dust with cocoa powder.*

# GOLDEN MOMENTS

*Pastry cakes and almond-rich marzipan*

## CROQUEMBOUCHE

*This tower of small choux puffs, each one filled with crème pâtissière, joined together with caramel and draped with spun sugar is a traditonal wedding cake of France. This recipe will make approximately 30 profiteroles or a tower about 40 cm (16 in) high.*

### PASTRY
*350 ml (12 ¼ fl oz) water*
*150 g (5 ¼ oz) unsalted butter*
*150 g (5 ¼ oz) plain (all-purpose) flour*
*5 x 60 g (2 oz, large) eggs, lightly beaten*

### FILLING
*500 ml (17 ½ fl oz) crème pâtissière (see page 165)*

### TO DECORATE
*250 ml (9 fl oz) caramel (see page 158)*

Preheat oven to 200 deg C (400 deg F). Line a baking tray (sheet) with baking parchment.

Place the water and butter in a saucepan and bring to the boil over medium heat. Remove from heat and add the flour all at once, beating all the time. Cook until the mixture leaves the sides of the saucepan, stirring all the time. Remove from the heat and gradually add the eggs until the mixture is smooth, soft and shiny. Use a piping (pastry) bag fitted with a plain nozzle to pipe small mounds about 2 ½ cm (1 in) high on the prepared tray. Bake for 20–25 minutes or until profiteroles are puffed, brown and crisp. Cool profiteroles on the tray on a wire rack. Use the piping bag to fill each profiterole with crème pâtissière.

### TO ASSEMBLE
Dip profiteroles into the caramel and position them side by side to form a ring. Keep adding profiteroles, reducing the number on each layer and stepping in each ring from the previous one to make a cone-shaped pyramid. Dip a fork into the remaining caramel and spin fine threads of caramel (see page 158) over the top of the Croquembouche.

**STEP ONE:** *Dip the profiteroles into the caramel and cover evenly.*

**STEP TWO:** *Make a small ring of filled and dipped profiteroles on a serving platter.*

**STEP THREE:** *Fill the middle of the ring with profiteroles.*

**STEP FOUR:** *Build up the stack, one layer at a time, starting on the outside edges and then filling in the centre.*

**STEP FIVE:** *Dip a fork into the remaining caramel and spin caramel threads over the Croquembouche.*

**STEP SIX:** *Spin the caramel threads over the Croquembouche until the desired decoration is achieved.*

# LINZER TORTE

This torte has its origins in the Austrian city of Linz. The rich sweet pastry base is spread with red currant jelly and decorated with strips of dough arranged in a lattice pattern.

250 g (9 oz) plain (all-purpose) flour
190 g (6 ¹/₂ oz) caster (superfine) sugar
150 g (5 ¹/₄ oz) ground almonds
190 g (6 ¹/₂ oz) unsalted butter, cut into small pieces
1 x 60 g (2 oz, large) egg, lightly beaten
juice of one lemon
25 ml (³/₄ fl oz) milk
125 g (4 ¹/₂ oz) red currant jelly
beaten egg wash (see page 167)

apricot glaze (see page 166)
fondant glaze (see page 166)

Preheat oven to 200 deg C (400 deg F). Grease the base of a 23 cm (9 in) spring form pan very lightly with butter.

Place the flour, sugar and the almonds in a bowl and mix lightly. Add the butter and very lightly rub into the flour until the mixture resembles fresh breadcrumbs. Add the egg, lemon juice and sufficient milk to make a firm dough. Wrap in plastic (cling) wrap and chill for 15 minutes.

Roll out three quarters of the dough into a 23 cm (9 in) circle and cover the prepared base. Brush top with red currant jelly. Roll out half of the remaining dough thinly. Cut into narrow strips with a fluted roller cutter and arrange in a lattice pattern on top of the jelly. Shape the remaining dough into a long sausage to fit around the edge of the pastry base. Trim ends to neaten and place in position. Brush with the egg wash, making sure that none of the egg drips on the jelly. Bake for 35–40 minutes or until the pastry is a light brown. When cool brush with apricot glaze and allow to dry before applying the fondant glaze.

# PITHIVIERS

This cake originated in the tiny village of Pithiviers, about 80 kilometres south of Paris, and was brought to the city by Marie Antoine Carême. Hidden in the pillow of puff pastry is a delightfully moist almond cream. Take care when cooking that the puff pastry does not overcook while the almond is still uncooked.

*500 g (17 ¹/₂ oz) puff pastry*

FILLING
*100 g (3 ¹/₂ oz) unsalted (sweet) butter*
*100 g (3 ¹/₂ oz) caster (superfine) sugar*
*1 egg yolk*
*30 g (1 oz) plain (all-purpose) flour*
*100 g (3 ¹/₂) ground almonds*
*beaten egg wash (see page 167)*

*apricot glaze (see page 166)*
*60 g (2 oz) flaked almonds, roasted (see page 171)*

Preheat oven to 180 deg C (350 deg F). Line a baking tray (sheet) with baking parchment. Roll out the pastry and cut two 23 cm (9 in) circles. Chill while preparing the filling.

Beat the butter and sugar until creamy, light and fluffy. Add the egg yolk and beat for 3 minutes. Beat in the flour and almonds.

Place one of the pastry circles on the prepared tray and brush a 4 cm (1 ¹/₂ in) border of egg wash around the edge of the pastry circle. Place the filling in the centre, keeping it inside the egg wash border, and shape it into a mound 2 cm (³/₄ in) high in the middle. Top with the second pastry circle. Crimp around the edge with the fingertips. Use a small sharp knife to lightly mark lines on the top of the pastry. Brush with beaten egg wash. Bake for 40 minutes or until both base and top are cooked. While hot, brush top and sides with apricot glaze and sprinkle sides with flaked almonds. Cool on the tray on a wire rack.

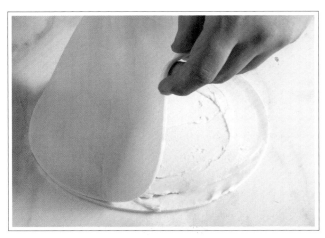

**STEP ONE:** *After the filling has been placed and shaped on the bottom layer of puff pastry, brush the edges with egg wash. Place the second layer of pastry on top.*

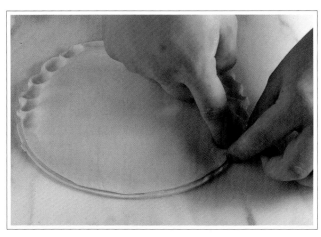

**STEP TWO:** *Use your fingers to pinch the edges of the pastry at regular intervals to give a decorative finish.*

**STEP THREE:** *With a small knife, lightly mark the top of the pastry with curved lines. Start in the centre and finish 1 cm (¹/₂ in) from the edge. Brush the top of the Pithiviers with egg wash and bake.*

# Vanilla Choux Gâteau

This superb creation of the pastry cook is also known as Snow Peak Gâteau. Under the sweet crunchy crust are layers of delicate vanilla sponge, heavenly white chocolate mousse and feathery light choux pastry.

### BASE
*105 g (3 ³/₄ oz) plain (all-purpose) flour*
*50 g (1 ³/₄ oz) icing (powdered) sugar*
*70 g (2 ¹/₂ oz) unsalted butter, cut into small pieces*
*1 x 60 g (2 oz, large) egg*

### PASTRY
*1 quantity choux pastry, uncooked (see page 117)*

### FILLING
*2 level teaspoons gelatine (gelatin)*
*3 teaspoons water*
*20 g (³/₄ oz) glucose (corn) syrup*
*2 egg yolks*
*200 g (7 oz) white chocolate, melted (see page 159)*
*350 ml (12 ¹/₄ fl oz) thickened (heavy or double) cream, lightly whipped*
*apricot jam*

*1 vanilla génoise sponge (see page 58), cut in half horizontally*

### TO SERVE
*icing (powdered) sugar*
*fresh fruit pieces*

### BASE
Place the flour and icing sugar in a bowl and very lightly rub in the butter until the mixture resembles coarse breadcrumbs. Add the egg and sufficient water to make a firm dough. Wrap in plastic (cling) wrap and chill for one hour.

Preheat oven to 180 deg C (350 deg F). Grease a 23 cm (9 in) round baking tray (sheet) lightly with butter and roll out the chilled dough to fit the prepared tray. Bake for 8–10 minutes or until light golden brown. Cool on the tray on a wire rack.

### PASTRY
Preheat oven to 200 deg C (400 deg F). Line two flat baking trays (sheets) with baking parchment and draw two 23 cm (9 in) circles on each. Use a piping (pastry) bag fitted with a plain 1 cm (¹/₂ in) nozzle to pipe two pastry rings onto the prepared trays. Bake for 25–30 minutes. Cool completely.

### FILLING
Mix the gelatine and water in a small bowl and stand the bowl in a pan of hot water. When the gelatine is dissolved, mix in the glucose syrup and warm slightly. Beat the mixture into the egg yolks and then mix in the chocolate. Cool. Fold in the whipped cream.

### TO ASSEMBLE
Brush the cooled pastry base with apricot jam and place a layer of sponge, cut side down, on top. Top with a choux ring and fill the centre with three quarters of the filling. Place the second layer of sponge, cut side down, on top. Freeze for 30 minutes.

Break the remaining ring into 1 cm (¹/₂ in) pieces. Cover the top and sides with the remaining filling. Press the choux pieces into the filling. Chill for one hour. Dust heavily with icing sugar and serve with fresh fruit pieces.

**STEP ONE:** *Pour the filling into the centre of the choux pastry ring.*

**STEP TWO:** *Top with the sponge layer. Cover with the extra filling and choux pastry pieces.*

# GÂTEAU SAINT HONORÉ

$T$his gâteau is named after the patron saint of pastry cooks and bakers, Saint Honoré.

### BASE
*100 g (3 ¹/₂ oz) plain (all-purpose) flour*
*50 g (1 ³/₄ oz) icing (powdered) sugar*
*70 g (2 ¹/₂ oz) unsalted butter, cut into small pieces*
*1 x 60 g (2 oz, large) egg, lightly beaten*

### CHOUX PASTRY
*300 ml (10 ¹/₂ fl oz) water*
*150 g (5 ¹/₄ oz) unsalted butter*
*150 g (5 ¹/₄ oz) plain (all-purpose) flour*
*5 x 60 g (2 oz, large) eggs, lightly beaten*
*beaten egg wash (see page 167)*
*apricot glaze (see page 166)*
*375 g (13 ¹/₄ oz) crème chiboust (see page 164)*
*300 ml (10 ¹/₂ fl oz) crème Chantilly (see page 164)*

### TO DECORATE
*125 ml (4 ¹/₂ fl oz) caramel (see page 158)*
*fresh fruit pieces*

### BASE
Preheat oven to 180 deg C (350 deg F). Grease the base of a 23 cm (9 in) spring form pan very lightly with butter.

Place the flour and icing sugar in a bowl. Add the butter and very lightly rub into the flour until the mixture resembles fresh breadcrumbs. Add the egg and mix to a firm dough. Wrap in plastic (cling) wrap and chill for 30 minutes. Roll out to fit the prepared base and prick all over with a fork. Bake for 10–12 minutes or until very lightly browned. Cool the pastry on the base on a wire rack.

### CHOUX PASTRY
Preheat oven to 200 deg C (400 deg F). Line a flat baking tray (sheet) with baking parchment.

Place the water and butter in a saucepan and bring to the boil over a medium heat. Remove from the heat and add the flour all at once, beating all the time. Cook until the mixture leaves the sides of the saucepan, stirring all the time. Remove from the heat and add the eggs, a little at a time, until the mixture is smooth, soft and shiny. Fill a piping bag fitted with a star-shaped nozzle and pipe a 23 cm (9 in)

doughnut-shaped ring and twelve 3 cm (1 ¹/₄ in) mounds onto the prepared tray. Brush with a little egg wash and bake for 25–30 minutes or until the profiteroles are puffed, brown and crisp. Cool the profiteroles on the tray on a wire rack.

### TO ASSEMBLE
Slide the cooled pastry base onto a serving dish and cover the top and sides with a thin layer of apricot glaze. Place the choux pastry ring on top. Spoon the crème chiboust into the centre of the ring and smooth. Cover with fresh fruit pieces. Fill a piping (pastry) bag fitted with a nozzle with crème Chantilly and pipe decoratively over the fruit. By lightly scoring the crème with a knife divide the gâteau into 12 wedges. Dip the profiteroles in lukewarm caramel and place around the edge of the ring with one profiterole per portion. Decorate with extra fruit pieces.

**STEP ONE:** *Place the choux pastry ring onto the pastry base and fill with the crème chiboust.*

**STEP TWO:** *Cover the crème chiboust with fresh fruits and crème Chantilly before placing caramel covered profiteroles around the edge of the gâteau.*

# OVERFLODIGSHORN

*This wonderful piece of abstract sculpture is a Danish wedding cake. Marzipan is the basic building material and some Overflodigshorn can rise to dizzy heights. This one is of more modest dimensions.*

**500 g (17 ¹/₂ oz) marzipan**
**300 g (10 ¹/₂ oz) caster (superfine) sugar**
**6 egg whites, lightly beaten**
**250 g (9 oz) dark (plain or semi-sweet) chocolate, melted (see page 159)**
**marzipan flowers for decoration(see page 170)**

Line two or three baking trays (sheets) with baking parchment.

Blend together the marzipan and sugar until they are well combined and have formed a solid mass. Add sufficient egg white to make a soft paste that can be piped without losing its shape. Fill a piping (pastry) bag fitted with a plain 1 cm (¹/₂ in) nozzle with the marzipan paste and, using different sized pastry cutters as a guide, pipe 10 rings of different sizes onto the prepared trays. Shape some marzipan into a ball the same size as the centre of the second smallest ring. Leave the rings out to dry for 8 hours.

Preheat oven to 160 deg C (320 deg F) and bake the rings for 10–15 minutes or until golden brown. Leave on the trays for 24 hours to dry.

### TO ASSEMBLE

Take the smallest ring and join to the next smallest with chocolate until all the rings are used. Secure the ball of marzipan on the top with more chocolate. The horn can either stand upright or can be curved by piping more chocolate on one side of the ring than the other (see photographs). A marzipan ball will need to support it underneath. Place the horn in a cold place, but do not refrigerate as the marzipan will 'sweat'.

Decorate with marzipan flowers. Fill a curved horn with petits fours.

**STEP ONE:** *Using a set of cutters, pipe marzipan rings onto the prepared trays.*

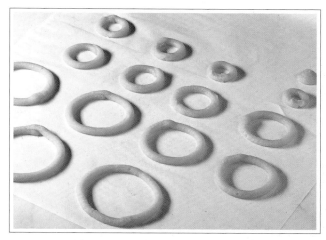

**STEP TWO:** *The rings should go from a large to a small sized ball.*

**STEP THREE:** *Bake the rings until they are golden brown.*

**STEP FOUR:** *Join the rings together with chocolate, piping it thicker at the back than the front so that the rings curve as they get higher.*

**STEP SIX:** *Join the largest two sets of rings first and allow to set hard.*

**STEP FIVE:** *Join the rings together in three piles and allow to set hard before joining them.*

**STEP SEVEN:** *Finally, join on the smallest set of rings to produce the horn. Allow to set before decorating.*

# PARIS BREST

*This Parisian speciality was created to commemorate the famous Paris to Brest bicycle race. The wheel of baked choux pastry is split and filled with crème Chantilly and fresh fruit.*

*375 ml (13 ¼ fl oz) water*
*190 g (6 ½ oz) unsalted butter*
*190 g (6 ½ oz) plain (all-purpose) flour*
*3 x 60 g (2 oz, large) eggs, lightly beaten*
*100 g (3 ½ oz) flaked almonds, roasted (see page 171)*
*crème Chantilly (see page 164)*
*fresh fruit pieces*
*icing (powdered) sugar for dusting*

Preheat oven to 200 deg C (400 deg F). Line a baking tray (sheet) with baking parchment and on it draw a 23 cm (9 in) circle.

Place the water and butter in a saucepan and bring to the boil over medium heat. Remove from the heat and add the flour all at once, beating all the time. Return the saucepan to the heat and cook until the mixture leaves the sides, stirring all the time. Remove from the heat and add the lightly beaten eggs a little at a time, until the mixture is smooth, soft and shiny. Fill a piping (pastry) bag fitted with a medium to large fluted nozzle with the mixture. Pipe a thick line of choux pastry onto the prepared tray following the outline of the circle. Sprinkle flaked almonds on the pastry. Bake for 35–40 minutes or until the choux pastry is a medium golden brown. Cool on the tray on a wire rack.

When cold cut in half horizontally and fill the bottom half with crème Chantilly and fresh fruit. Replace the top and dust with icing sugar.

# LIGHT *and* LUSCIOUS

*Creamy cheesecakes — dreamy mousse-filled sponges — delicate meringues*

## CHOCOLATE DELICE

T*he name says it all. It is a truly delicious gâteau with a white chocolate mousse filling and dark chocolate coating resting on a sweet almond base.*

#### BASE
*90 g (3 oz) unsalted butter*
*90 g (3 oz) caster (superfine) sugar*
*2 x 60 g (2 oz, large) eggs*
*90 g (3 oz) ground almonds*
*30 g (1 oz) plain (all-purpose) flour*
*2 level teaspoons cornflour (cornstarch)*

#### FILLING
*3 level teaspoons gelatine (gelatin)*
*30 ml (1 fl oz) water*
*30 g (1 oz) glucose (corn) syrup*
*30 ml (1 fl oz) water, extra*
*3 egg yolks*
*300 g (10 1/2 oz) white chocolate, melted (see page 159)*
*550 ml (19 1/2 fl oz) thickened (double or heavy) cream, whipped*

#### TOPPING
*3 level teaspoons gelatine (gelatin)*
*125 ml (4 1/2 fl oz) water*
*60 g (2 oz) caster (superfine) sugar*
*60 g (2 oz) dark (plain or semi-sweet) chocolate, finely chopped*

*40 ml (1 1/2 fl oz) water, extra*
*30 g (1 oz) cocoa powder*
*45 g (1 1/2 oz) caster (superfine) sugar, extra*
*2 level teaspoons cornflour (cornstarch)*

#### BASE
Preheat oven to 180 deg C (350 deg F). Line a baking tray (sheet) with baking parchment.

Beat the butter and sugar until creamy, light and fluffy. Add the eggs one at a time and beat well after each one is added. Fold in by hand the almonds and the flours. Pour the mixture into the prepared tray and bake for 5–8 minutes or until the cake is lightly browned and the top springs back when lightly touched. Cool in the tray. When cool, cut a 23 cm (9 in) circle using the inside edge of the rim of a spring form pan as a guide. Place the cut cake in the bottom of a spring form pan.

#### FILLING
Mix the gelatine and water in a small bowl. Stand the bowl in a pan of hot water until the gelatine dissolves. Heat the glucose syrup and extra water in a saucepan and blend into the dissolved gelatine. Allow to cool slightly. Place the egg yolks in a bowl, add the gelatine mixture and whisk. Whisk in the white chocolate and very gently but quickly fold in the whipped cream. Pour onto the base, smooth the surface and refrigerate for 2 hours or until set.

## TOPPING

Mix the gelatine and 4 teaspoons of the water in a small bowl. Stand the bowl in a pan of hot water until the gelatine is dissolved. Put the remaining water, sugar and dark chocolate in a saucepan and bring to the boil, stirring all the time. Blend the extra water, cocoa powder, extra sugar and cornflour and stir into the hot mixture, stirring all the time. Remove from the heat and mix in the dissolved gelatine. Cool.

When the topping is cold, slowly pour it onto the mousse. Chill for one hour before removing from the pan.

**STEP THREE:** *When the topping has set, run a hot knife around the edge of the cake pan.*

**STEP ONE:** *When the white chocolate filling has set, remove it from the refrigerator.*

**STEP FOUR:** *Carefully remove the cake ring.*

**STEP TWO:** *Pour the cooled topping over the base. Work quickly to ensure the topping covers the entire base before setting. Remove any air bubbles with a toothpick or sharp knife. Place in refrigerator to set.*

# CHEESECAKE

*The cheesecake has evolved into many forms and this one, an unbaked version with a filling of sweetened cream cheese, eggs and cream, has become very popular because it is so easy to prepare.*

**250 g (9 oz) sweet plain biscuit (cookie or cracker) crumbs**
**100 g (3 ¹/₂ oz) unsalted butter, melted**

FILLING
**350 g (12 ¹/₄ oz) packet cream cheese**
**150 g (5 ¹/₄ oz) caster (superfine) sugar**
**4 x 60 g (2 oz, large) eggs**
**6 level teaspoons gelatine (gelatin)**
**4 teaspoons water**
**juice and grated rind of 2 lemons**
**300 ml (10 ¹/₂ fl oz) thickened (double or heavy) cream, whipped**
**ground cinnamon for dusting**

Line a 23 cm (9 in) spring form pan with plastic (cling) wrap.

Mix crumbs and butter and press into the pan using the back of a spoon to make a firm, flat base. Chill.

Beat the cream cheese and sugar until light and creamy then beat in the eggs one at a time. Mix the gelatine and cold water in a small bowl and let stand for 3 minutes. Heat the lemon juice until just boiling and add the soaked gelatine. Remove from the heat and stir until the gelatine dissolves. Add the rind. When cool, beat the gelatine mixture and creamed ingredients. Gently fold in by hand the whipped cream. Pour over the chilled base and refrigerate for at least 2 hours or until set. Turn the cake out and peel off the plastic wrap.

Lightly dust the top with cinnamon.

# PAVLOVA

T*he Pavlova was created in 1935 by an Australian chef, Herbert Sachse, who wanted to make a soft meringue cake to be served at a special afternoon tea in the hotel where he worked. The cake was so light that it was named after the ballerina Anna Pavlova who had visited Australia in the 1920s. This recipe makes a crunchy, not a soft-centred Pavlova.*

*8 egg whites*
*500 g (17 ¹/₂ oz) caster (superfine) sugar*
*1 ¹/₂  teaspoons white vinegar*
*vanilla essence (extract)*
*300 ml (10 ¹/₂ oz) crème Chantilly (see page 164)*
*fresh fruit pieces dusted with icing (powdered) sugar*

Preheat oven to 100 deg C (210 deg F). Line a baking tray (sheet) with baking parchment and draw a 23 cm (9 in) circle on it.

Beat the egg whites until stiff peaks form (see page 173) and gradually beat in the sugar a spoonful at a time. Beat until the sugar is dissolved. Add the vinegar and vanilla essence and beat for one minute. Spread the mixture inside the marked circle on the prepared tray and bake for 1 ³/₄ hours. Turn off the oven, open the door slightly and leave the Pavlova in the oven until completely cold. Place on a serving platter and just prior to serving, cover the top with crème Chantilly and fruit pieces.

**STEP ONE:** *The Pavlova must be finished with its crème Chantilly and fresh fruits just prior to serving. Ensure that all fruits and the crème are ready beforehand.*

**STEP TWO:** *To decorate, cover the top surface of the Pavlova with the crème Chantilly and spread  evenly.*

**STEP THREE:** *The fruit decoration can be as exotic as you like, but have a plan before beginning. Once the fruit is on the crème, it is hard and messy to remove.*

# STRAWBERRY MOUSSE CAKE

*This is the perfect cake to end a long lazy lunch on a warm summer day. The flavours of strawberries and orange juice blend beautifully in the layers of cake and mousse filling.*

*75 g (2 ¹/₂ oz) plain (all-purpose) flour*
*45 g (1 ¹/₂ oz) cornflour (cornstarch)*
*5 egg yolks*
*155 g (5 ¹/₂ oz) caster (superfine) sugar*
*75 g (2 ¹/₂ oz) grated orange rind*
*100 ml (3 ¹/₂ fl oz) freshly squeezed orange juice*
*30 ml (1 fl oz) Grand Marnier*
*100 g (3 ¹/₂ oz) marzipan*
*5 egg whites*
*50 g (1 ³/₄ oz) caster (superfine) sugar, extra*

### FILLING
*350 g (12 ¹/₄ oz) strawberries, hulled and coarsely chopped*
*60 ml (2 fl oz) Grand Marnier*
*6 egg yolks*
*120 g (4 ¹/₄ oz) caster (superfine) sugar*
*250 ml (9 fl oz) milk*
*10 level teaspoons gelatine (gelatin)*
*60 ml (2 fl oz) water*
*180 ml (6 ¹/₄ fl oz) freshly squeezed orange juice*
*500 ml (17 ¹/₂ fl oz) thickened (double or heavy) cream, lightly whipped*

### TO DECORATE
*strawberries, extra*
*200 ml (7 fl oz) strawberry glaze (see page 166)*
*100 g (3 ¹/₂ oz) flaked almonds*

Preheat oven to 180 deg C (350 deg F). Grease a 23 cm (9 in) spring form pan lightly with butter and line sides and base with baking parchment. Sift the flours twice.

Beat egg yolks and sugar until thick and pale and the mixture forms a ribbon (see page 172). While the egg yolks are beating, place the orange rind, juice, Grand Marnier and marzipan in a saucepan and slowly bring to the boil, stirring all the time, until the marzipan breaks down and the mixture is smooth. Allow to cool slightly. Beat the egg whites until stiff peaks form (see page 173) and gradually beat in the extra sugar a spoonful at a time.

Fold by hand the beaten egg yolks into the boiled marzipan mixture and gently fold in the sifted flours. Fold in the beaten egg whites. Pour into the prepared pan and bake for 35–40 minutes or until the cake has shrunk a little away from the sides of the pan and the top of the cake springs back when lightly touched. Cool in the pan on a wire rack.

### FILLING
Soak the strawberries in the Grand Marnier for one hour. Place the egg yolks, sugar and milk in a heatproof bowl and place over a saucepan of simmering water. Heat until barely warmed.

Mix the gelatine and water in a small bowl.

Place the orange juice in a saucepan and bring to the boil. Add the soaked gelatine and stir until dissolved. Cool slightly and add to the egg yolk mixture. Chill and allow to thicken slightly. Fold in the strawberries soaked in Grand Marnier and the whipped cream.

### TO ASSEMBLE
When the cake is cold remove from the pan and cut into quarters horizontally. Place one layer in the pan and spread with a quarter of the filling. Repeat with the remaining layers of cake and filling. Chill the cake for 2 hours. Decorate the top of the cake with the extra strawberries and brush with the strawberry glaze. Chill for another hour before removing from the pan. Press flaked almonds around the side of the cake.

# CHOCOLATE MARQUISE TORTE

*Allow yourself plenty of time to make this torte. Prepare the filling the day before, cut the baking parchment accurately, and be sure to allow enough time for chilling. Is it worth all the trouble? Yes!*

### FILLING
*700 ml (24 ¹/₂ fl oz) cream (single or light)*
*180 g (6 ¹/₄ oz) white chocolate, chopped*
*360 g (12 ¹/₂ oz) dark (plain or semi-sweet) chocolate, chopped*

### CAKE
*12 level teaspoons instant coffee*
*60 ml (2 fl oz) water*
*6 egg yolks*
*180 g (6 ¹/₄ oz) dark (plain or semi-sweet) chocolate, chopped*
*6 egg whites*
*130 g (4 ¹/₂ oz) caster (superfine) sugar*
*cocoa powder for dusting*

### FILLING
Make the filling the day before you make the cake.

Heat the cream in a small saucepan. Remove from the heat and add all the chocolate. Stir until the chocolate melts. Cool, cover and refrigerate for 24 hours.

### CAKE
Preheat oven to 180 deg C (350 deg F). Line a 35 cm x 30 cm (14 in x 12 in) baking tray (sheet) with baking parchment.

Dissolve the instant coffee in the water and blend into the egg yolks. Place the chocolate in a bowl and melt over hot water. Cool slightly and mix into the coffee mixture. Beat the egg whites until stiff peaks form (see page 173), then gradually beat in the sugar a spoonful at a time. Beat until the sugar is dissolved. Take a spoonful of the beaten egg whites and mix by hand into the coffee mixture. Gently fold in the remaining beaten egg whites. Spread the mixture very thinly into the prepared tray and bake for 10–12 minutes or until the top of the cake springs back when lightly touched. Turn the cake out onto a wire rack to cool.

### TO ASSEMBLE
Line a 7 cm x 25 cm x 5 cm (2 ³/₄ in x 10 in x 2 in) bar or loaf pan with baking parchment. Cut three rectangles of cake the same size as the base of the pan and two rectangles to line the two long sides of the prepared pan.

Line the base and sides with the appropriate rectangles of cake. Whip the chilled chocolate filling until it thickens and carefully spoon half the mixture into the prepared pan. Use a small palette knife to spread the mixture into the corners. Smooth. Top with another rectangle of cake and carefully spoon the remaining filling into the pan. Top with the remaining rectangle of cake and press down lightly. Refrigerate for 4 hours.

To serve, turn out the torte onto a serving platter, peel off the baking parchment and dust the top with cocoa powder. Cut with a hot knife and use a smooth cutting action.

**STEP ONE:** *Whip the chocolate filling until thick, smooth and spreading consistency.*

**STEP TWO:** *Line the base and the two longest sides of the pan with strips of cake.*

**STEP THREE:** *Place half of the filling mixture into the lined pan.*

**STEP FOUR:** *Use a palette knife to spread the filling into the corners and smooth the surface.*

**STEP FIVE:** *Place another strip of cake on top of the filling mixture. Remove the baking parchment and press the cake onto the filling.*

**STEP SIX:** *Place the other half of the filling mixture into the pan.*

**STEP SEVEN:** *Use a palette knife to spread the mixture into the corners and ensure the surface is smooth.*

**STEP EIGHT:** *Place the last strip of cake on top of the filling and press so that it is held firmly by the mixture. Remove the paper and chill.*

# Tirami-sù

Tirami-sù means 'pick me up' and this cake owes its name to the reviving influence of the coffee liqueur. This Italian torta is a relatively new addition to the cake world and has become an instant celebrity.

### Filling
7 level teaspoons gelatine (gelatin)
60 ml (2 fl oz) water
125 ml (4 ½ fl oz) coffee liqueur
125 g (4 ½ oz) caster (superfine) sugar
60 g (2 oz) instant coffee
500 g (17 ½ oz) mascapone (mascherpone)
3 x 60 g (2 oz, large) eggs
250 ml (9 fl oz) thickened (double or heavy) cream,
lightly whipped
2 japonaise bases (see page 57)
cocoa powder for dusting

Place the gelatine and water in a small bowl and stand in a pan of hot water to dissolve. Place the coffee liqueur, sugar and instant coffee in a saucepan and bring to the boil. Stir in the dissolved gelatine. Place the mascapone in a mixing bowl and beat in the eggs and coffee mixture. Gently fold in the whipped cream.

Place one of the japonaise bases in the bottom of a 23 cm (9 in) spring form pan and pour in the mixture. Top with the second base and press down lightly. Chill for 2 hours. Remove from the pan and dust the top with cocoa powder.

# HAZELNUT AND
# HONEY TORTE

*A silky smooth filling contrasts dramatically with
the crunchy roasted hazelnut topping.*

### BASE
*160 g (5 ¹/₂ oz) plain (all-purpose) flour
90 g (3 oz) icing (powdered) sugar
100 g (3 ¹/₂ oz) unsalted butter, cut into small pieces
1 x 60 g (2 oz, large) egg, lightly beaten
2 teaspoons water*

### FILLING
*9 x 60 g (2 oz, large) eggs
525 ml (18 ¹/₄ fl oz) cream (single or light)
230 ml (8 fl oz) honey
90 g (3 oz) caster (superfine) sugar*

### TO DECORATE
*300 g (10 ¹/₂ oz) chopped hazelnuts, roasted
apricot glaze (see page 166)*

Place the flour and icing sugar in a bowl and very
lightly rub in the butter until the mixture resembles
coarse breadcrumbs. Add the egg and sufficient
water to make a firm dough. Wrap in plastic (cling)
wrap and chill for one hour.

Grease a 23 cm (9 in) spring form pan. Preheat
oven to 170 deg C (340 deg F). Roll out the chilled
dough into a 27 cm (10 ³/₄ in) circle and line the
base and sides of the prepared pan.

Beat the eggs, cream, honey and sugar until
thoroughly mixed and pour into the prepared pan.
Bake for 25 minutes. Remove from the oven and
lightly press roasted hazelnuts into the surface of the
filling. Bake for another 15 minutes or until golden
brown and firm to the touch. Cool in the pan for 5
minutes before removing the rim of the pan. Cool on
a wire rack. When cold, brush the top with apricot
glaze.

# DANISH ALMONDINE

$T$his almond torte with its crunchy exterior and a soft heart of creamy filling, is at its very best on the day it is made.

2 japonaise bases (see page 57)

FILLING
3 teaspoons gelatine (gelatin)
60 ml (2 fl oz) cold water
450 ml (16 fl oz) cream (single or light)
175 g (6 1/4 oz) caster (superfine) sugar
130 g (4 1/2 oz) unsalted butter, softened
7 egg yolks
1 quantity praline, crushed (see page 158)

TO DECORATE
250 g (9 oz) marzipan (see page 168)
100 g (3 1/2 oz) flaked almonds, roasted (see page 171)

Mix the gelatine and water in a small bowl and allow to soak in. Place the cream, sugar and butter in a saucepan and bring to the boil. Remove from the heat and add gelatine. Stir until dissolved. Beat the egg yolks lightly and add to the mixture, beating all the time. Cook the mixture over a low heat until it thickens, stirring all the time. Do not boil. Remove from heat and cool. Add the praline. Spread three quarters of the filling onto one of the japonaise bases. Top with the second base and cover the top and sides of the cake with the remaining filling. Sprinkle the almonds over the top of the cake. Roll out the marzipan thinly and cut a strip to fit around the side of the cake. For extra effect texture the marzipan with a patterned rolling pin.

# CHARLOTTE RUSSE

*M*arie Antoine Carême, founder of classic French cookery, created the first Charlotte Russe in 1915 and its invention was somewhat of an accident. When Carême found he did not have quite enough gelatine to hold up one of his desserts he improvised using sponge fingers to support the sides and **voila**! Charlotte Russe.

### SPONGE FINGERS
*115 g (4 oz) plain (all-purpose) flour*
*5 egg yolks*
*115 g (4 oz) caster (superfine) sugar*
*5 egg whites*
*(or 1 packet of 24 Savoiardi, sponge finger or lady finger biscuits)*

### FILLING
*8 level teaspoons gelatine (gelatin)*
*90 ml (3 fl oz) cold water*
*550 ml (19 1/2 fl oz) milk*
*1 vanilla bean*
*6 egg yolks*
*180 g (6 1/4 oz) caster (superfine) sugar*
*250 ml (9 fl oz) thickened (double or heavy) cream, whipped*
*200 ml (7 fl oz) passionfruit (purple granadilla) pulp*

### TO DECORATE
*100 ml (3 1/2 fl oz) passionfruit (purple granadilla) pulp, reserved*
*ribbon to tie around cake*

Preheat oven to 180 deg C (350 deg F). Line a baking tray (sheet) with baking parchment. Sift the flour twice. Beat the egg yolks and sugar until thick, light and fluffy and the mixture forms a ribbon (see page 172). Beat the egg whites until stiff peaks form (see page 173). Fold the sifted flour into the egg yolks. Very gently fold in the beaten egg whites. Fill a piping (pastry) bag fitted with a plain 1 cm (1/2 in) nozzle with the mixture and pipe 10 cm (4 in) lines onto the prepared tray leaving 4 cm (1 1/2 in) between each line. Bake for 10–15 minutes or until the top springs back when lightly touched. Cool on the tray on a wire rack.

### FILLING
Mix the gelatine and the water in a small bowl. Stand the bowl in a pan of hot water to dissolve the gelatine.

Place the milk and the vanilla bean in a saucepan and bring slowly to the boil.

Beat the egg yolks and the sugar together and very slowly beat in the boiling milk. Return the mixture to the milk saucepan and cook over a very low heat until the mixture thickens, stirring all the time. Remove from heat and mix in the dissolved gelatine. Cool until slightly thickened. Remove the vanilla bean. Mix the whipped cream and one third of the passionfruit pulp together and fold into the thickened mixture.

### TO ASSEMBLE
Line the base and sides of a 23 cm (9 in) spring form pan with the sponge fingers, trimming them to fit. Pour the mousse filling into the pan. Tap the pan lightly on the bench (counter) to bring any large air bubbles to the top. Chill for 1–2 hours or until completely set.

To serve remove the pan and tie a ribbon around the side. Spoon the reserved passionfruit pulp on top.

# DAY AND NIGHT MOUSSE CAKE

*This is a cake to enjoy at any time of the day or night. It takes its name from the contrasting layers of white and dark mousse fillings.*

*1 chocolate génoise sponge (see page 59)*

### FILLING (WHITE MOUSSE)
*4 level teaspoons gelatine (gelatin)*
*30 ml (1 fl oz) water*
*100 g (3 1/2 oz) white chocolate, chopped*
*3 egg yolks*
*150 ml (5 1/4 fl oz) cream (single or light)*
*60 g (2 oz) sugar*
*150 ml (5 1/4 fl oz) thickened cream (double or heavy), whipped*
*3 egg whites*

### FILLING (DARK MOUSSE)
*4 level teaspoons gelatine (gelatin)*
*30 ml (1 fl oz) water*
*100 g (3 1/2 oz) dark (plain or semi-sweet) chocolate, chopped*
*3 egg yolks*
*150 ml (5 1/4 fl oz) cream (single or light)*
*60 g (2 oz) sugar*
*150 ml (5 1/4 fl oz) thickened cream (double or heavy), whipped*
*3 egg whites*

### TO DECORATE
*400 g (14 oz) marzipan (see page 168)*
*100 g (3 1/2 oz) dark (plain or semi-sweet) chocolate, melted (see page 159)*

Cut the sponge in half horizontally and place one half in the base of a 23 cm (9 in) spring form pan. The method for making both mousses is exactly the same. Mix the gelatine and water in a small bowl. Stand the bowl in a pan of hot water until the gelatine is dissolved. Place the chocolate in the top half of a double boiler and melt slowly over hot water, stirring occasionally. Remove from heat and allow chocolate to cool slightly.

Place the egg yolks, cream and sugar in a heatproof bowl and whisk until blended. Stand the bowl on a wire rack over a saucepan of simmering water. Do not let the bottom of the bowl touch the hot water. Beat the mixture until it thickens. Mix the gelatine into the egg yolks, making sure that both are the same temperature. Blend in the melted chocolate. Cool over ice, stirring occasionally. When cooled and thickened, remove from ice and fold in by hand the whipped cream. Beat the egg whites until soft peaks form (see page 173) and gently fold into the chocolate mixture.

Pour half of the white chocolate mousse into the prepared pan and freeze for 10 minutes or until slightly firm. Repeat procedure with the remaining mousses. Place the second layer of sponge on top and freeze the cake for 20 minutes or until set. Remove from freezer and refrigerate for 2 hours. Roll out the marzipan thinly. For extra effect texture the marzipan with a patterned rolling pin. Cover the top and sides of the cake with the marzipan and trim the edges. Using a pastry brush, paint thinly with melted chocolate.

**STEP ONE:** *Layer the mousses alternately, chilling each layer separately.*

**STEP TWO:** *When all the mousse mixture has been used, place a layer of sponge on top.*

**STEP THREE:** *Chill the cake until firm. Cover the cake with a thin layer of marzipan. Use a pastry brush to paint thinly with melted chocolate.*

# BAKED CHEESECAKE

Greeks claim to have created the very first Cheesecake using cottage cheese, eggs and honey. This version of a traditional favourite is as light as a feather and will melt in your mouth.

300 ml (10 1/2 fl oz) milk
30 g (1 oz) butter
250 g (9 oz) cream cheese
30 g (1 oz) sugar
125 ml (4 1/2 fl oz) milk, extra
60 g (2 oz) custard powder
6 egg whites
100 g (3 1/2 oz) caster (superfine) sugar
60 g (2 oz) flaked almonds, roasted, (see page 171) to decorate

Preheat oven to 180 deg C (350 deg F). Grease a 23 cm (9 in) spring form pan lightly with butter and line the base with baking parchment.

Place the milk, butter, cream cheese and sugar in a saucepan and bring slowly to the boil. Blend the extra milk and custard powder and beat into the mixture as it heats. Cook until thickened, stirring all the time. Remove from the heat and cool slightly.

Beat the egg whites until stiff peaks form (see page 173) then gradually beat in the caster sugar a spoonful at a time. Beat until the sugar is dissolved. Fold by hand into the custard mixture and pour into the prepared pan. Bake for 25–30 minutes or until just cooked. Cool in the pan on a wire rack.

When cold run a knife around the edge of the pan to loosen the cake. Press flaked almonds around the side of the cake.

# RICHLY RUSTIC

*Plain and fruity yeast cakes
from around the world*

## BIENENSTICH

B*ienenstich is German for 'bee sting' and the
story goes that on the day the cake was first made,
the baker was stung by a bee attracted by the honey
glaze he was brushing on the finished cake.*

### CAKE
*30 g (1 oz) fresh compressed (active dry) yeast
(see page 172)
45 g (1 1/2 oz) butter, softened
45 g (1 1/2 oz) sugar
345 g (12 1/4 oz) plain (all-purpose) flour
1/8 level teaspoon salt
cold water*

### TOPPING
*125 g (4 1/2 oz) unsalted butter
125 g (4 1/2 oz) caster (superfine) sugar
60 g (2 oz) honey
125 g (4 1/2 oz) flaked almonds*

### FILLING
*500 ml (17 1/2 fl oz) confectioner's custard
(see page 164)*

Mix the yeast, butter, sugar, flour and salt using an
electric mixer fitted with a dough hook. Add
sufficient cold water to make a soft dough. Beat
slowly for 10 minutes. Cover and leave for 20 minutes
in a warm spot.

Grease a 23 cm (9 in) spring form pan lightly
with butter and line the base with baking parchment.

Place all the topping ingredients in a saucepan
and slowly bring to the boil. Boil for 2 minutes or
until the mixture leaves the sides of the saucepan.

Uncover the dough and knead lightly to expel
the air. Roll out into a 23 cm (9 in) circle and place
in the prepared pan.

Using a palette knife, spread the warm topping
over the dough. Place the pan in a warm spot and
allow to prove for 30–40 minutes or until the dough
has tripled and almost fills the pan. Preheat oven to
180 deg C (350 deg F). Bake for 35–40 minutes or
until a skewer inserted into the centre of the cake
comes out dry. Cool in the pan on a wire rack.

When cold, remove from the pan and cut in half
horizontally. Spread the bottom layer with
confectioner's custard and place the other layer on
top. Chill for one hour.

# GUGELHUPF

There are many versions of this cake but a true
Gugelhupf is baked in a fluted ring pan. In
Europe children often have it on their Name Day,
which is the birth day of the saint for whom they
were named.

### STARTER DOUGH
*(to be made the day before)*

*40 g (1 1/2 oz) fresh compressed (active dry) yeast (see
page 172)*
*250 ml (9 fl oz) lukewarm milk*
*280 g (10 oz) plain (all-purpose) flour*

### CAKE

*250 g (9 oz) unsalted butter*
*150 g (5 1/4 oz) caster (superfine) sugar*
*8 egg yolks*
*280 g (10 oz) plain (all-purpose) flour*
*150 g (5 1/4 oz) sultanas (golden raisins)*
*60 g (2 oz) blanched almonds, chopped*
*icing (powdered) sugar for dusting*

Mix the yeast and the milk. Place the flour in a bowl
and make a well in the centre. Pour the yeast mixture
into the well and gradually mix in the flour. Cover
the bowl with plastic (cling) wrap and leave in the
refrigerator for 8 hours.

Preheat oven to 180 deg C (350 deg F). Grease a
Guglehupf pan or any fancy fluted mould thoroughly
with butter and lightly dust with plain flour. Shake
out any excess.

Beat the butter and sugar until creamy, light and
fluffy. Add the egg yolks one at a time, beating very
well after each one is added. Mix in the starter
dough, flour, sultanas and chopped almonds. Pour
into the prepared mould, filling it only two thirds
full. Cover with a clean dry cloth and stand in a warm
place for 30 minutes. Bake for 35–40 minutes or until
a thin skewer inserted in the centre of the cake
comes out dry. Cool in the pan for 5 minutes before
turning out onto a wire rack.

Serve dusted with icing sugar.

# SAVARIN

$T$ *he Savarin is named after Jean Brillat-Savarin,*
*one of the gastronomic gurus of French cuisine*
*whose views on food and eating helped shape*
*classic French cooking styles.*

*500 g (17 ¹/₂ oz) bread (strong white) flour*
*¹/₄ teaspoon salt*
*30 g (1 oz) fresh compressed (active dry) yeast (see*
*page 172)*
*120 ml (4 ¹/₄ fl oz) lukewarm milk*
*6 x 60 g (2 oz, large) eggs, lightly beaten*
*30 g (1 oz) sugar*
*250 g (9 oz) unsalted butter, cut into*
*2 ¹/₂ cm (1 in) cubes*

SYRUP
*500 ml (17 ¹/₂ fl oz) water*
*300 g (10 ¹/₂) sugar*
*200 ml (7 fl oz) white (light) rum*
*cinnamon stick*
*5 whole cloves*

*fresh fruit pieces*
*icing (powdered) sugar for dusting*

Preheat oven to 180 deg C (350 deg F). Grease a 23 cm (9 in) Savarin (ring mold) pan very lightly with butter. Mix the flour and salt and sift twice.

Dissolve the yeast and milk in a large mixing bowl. Add the eggs and sugar and beat in the sifted flour and salt. Knead for 5 minutes. Place the butter on top of the dough and cover with a damp cloth. Leave the covered dough in a warm place to prove for 20 minutes. Beat in the butter. Place the dough in the prepared pan in a warm place and cover with a damp cloth for 30 minutes or until the dough has risen to the top of the pan. Bake for 45–50 minutes or until a skewer inserted in the centre of the cake comes out dry. Turn out onto a wire rack to cool.

Place all the ingredients for the syrup in a saucepan and bring to the boil. Simmer for 20 minutes. Place the cooled Savarin in a bowl and pour on the warm syrup. Leave until all the syrup has been absorbed by the Savarin.

To serve, fill the centre with fresh fruit pieces. Dust with icing sugar.

# HEFETEIG

This rich yeast cake was first made in Germany and Austria and though it is possible to beat it by hand an electric mixer makes light work of this recipe.

30 g (1 oz) fresh compressed (active dry) yeast
(see page 172)
60 g (2 oz) unsalted butter
60 g (2 oz) caster (superfine) sugar
425 g (14 ³/4 oz) plain (all-purpose) flour
¹/8 level teaspoon salt
30 g (1 oz) dried (dehydrated) milk powder
lukewarm water
150 g (5 ¹/4 oz) canned or fresh apricot halves

TO DECORATE
apricot glaze (see page 166)
100 g (3 ¹/2 oz) flaked almonds

Place the yeast, butter, sugar, flour, salt and milk powder in the bowl of an electric mixer fitted with a dough hook and blend for one minute. Gradually add the water in small amounts until the ingredients come together to form a soft dough. Add a little more water if necessary. Mix for 5 minutes. Cover and leave in a warm place to prove for 20 minutes.

Preheat oven to 180 deg C ( 350 deg F). Grease a 23 cm (9 in) spring form pan lightly with butter. Line the base with baking parchment.

Gently knead the dough for 30 seconds to expel the air. Roll out the dough into a 27 cm (10 ¹/2 in) circle and line the base and sides of the prepared pan. Top the dough with the apricot halves. Cover the pan with a clean dry cloth and leave in a warm place to prove for another 30 minutes. Bake for 40–45 minutes or until a skewer inserted in the centre of the cake comes out dry. Cool in the pan on a wire rack.

Turn the cake out of the pan and brush the top with apricot glaze. Press flaked almonds into the glazed top.

EASTER 03

# KULICH ✓

*Kulich is a rich brioche style sweet bread which contains dried fruits.*

*15 g (¹/₂ oz) fresh compressed (active dry) yeast (see page 172)*
*200 ml (7 fl oz) lukewarm milk*
*350 g (12 ¹/₄ oz) plain (all-purpose) flour*
*3 x 60 g (2 oz, large) eggs*
*135 g (4 ³/₄ oz) unsalted butter, softened*
*60 g (2 oz) sugar*
*70 g (2 ¹/₂ oz) mixed dried fruit*
*35 g (1 ¹/₄ oz) dried apricots, chopped*
*10 g (¹/₄ oz) mixed (candied) peel, chopped*

### TO DECORATE
*water icing (see page 168)*
*chopped nuts for decoration*

Dissolve the yeast in the milk in a small bowl. Place the flour into a large bowl. Make a well in the centre of the flour and add the dissolved yeast and eggs. Mix the ingredients together. Knead on a lightly floured board or in the bowl for 10 minutes. Place butter and sugar on top of the dough and stand the bowl in a warm place for 20 minutes. The dough will have doubled in bulk. Knock back the dough and beat in the butter and sugar until combined. Cover and refrigerate for 24 hours.

Preheat oven to 180 deg C (350 deg F). Grease a Kulich or fluted round pan lightly with butter and cut a circle of baking parchment to line the base.

Mix the dried fruit, apricots and chopped peel into the dough and knead for one minute. Place into the prepared pan, filling it only two thirds full. Cover with a clean dry cloth and stand in a warm place until the dough reaches the top of the pan. Bake for 35–40 minutes or until a skewer inserted into the centre of the cake comes out dry. Turn out onto a wire rack to cool.

When cold drizzle water icing over the top and sprinkle with chopped nuts.

# TOPPINGS
## *and*
# FILLINGS

## BUTTERCREAMS

Many recipes in this book suggest the buttercream most commonly used. However, any of the following buttercream recipes can be used in place of another.

Simple or more complicated, light or rich, it is only by experimenting that you will discover which recipe you prefer.

**STORAGE:** It is best to use buttercream as soon as it is made, when it is light, airy and fresh. If buttercream has to be stored it should be kept in an airtight container in the refrigerator. Remove from the refrigerator when required and stand at room temperature for one hour to soften. Beat in a mixing bowl until light and fluffy.

Never make more buttercream than is required to save time on the next cake. It is quicker to make it fresh than to reconstitute chilled buttercream.

Never store buttercream for more than two weeks in the refrigerator.

Each of the following recipes for buttercream is sufficient to decorate a single cake.

### FRENCH BUTTERCREAM

*A heavy, rich buttercream*

> *450 g (16 oz) unsalted butter*
> *160 g (5 ¹/₂ oz) fondant, softened*
> *3 x 60 g (2 oz, large) eggs*

Place the butter and fondant into a mixing bowl and beat until white, fluffy and smooth. Add the eggs one at a time and beat until thoroughly mixed.
Makes 690 g (24 ¹/₂ oz)

## CHOCOLATE FRENCH BUTTERCREAM

Melt 100 g (3 ¹/₂ oz) dark (plain or semi-sweet) chocolate. Add to the buttercream mixture. Cool the chocolate before adding to the mixture or the butter will melt and the buttercream will not become fluffy.

### QUICK NO-FUSS BUTTERCREAM

*A light variety which should please most*

> *400 g (14 oz) unsalted butter*
> *170 g (6 oz) icing (powdered) sugar*
> *3 x 60 g (2 oz, large) eggs*
> *2 teaspoons vanilla essence (extract)*

Beat the butter and icing sugar together until blended. Add the eggs one at a time beating well after each one is added. Add the essence and beat for 20 minutes at medium speed until the mixture is light and creamy.
Makes 660 g (23 ¹/₄ oz)

### CHOCOLATE BUTTERCREAM

After the butter, icing sugar, eggs and essence have been mixed together, blend 100 g (3 ¹/₂ oz) cooled, melted dark (plain or semi-sweet) chocolate to the mixture and beat for 20 minutes at medium speed.

### ORANGE BUTTERCREAM

Add the zest of 2 oranges and 60 ml (2 fl oz) of orange juice to the butter and icing sugar mixture and mix for 5 minutes at medium speed before adding the eggs. Use only one teaspoon of essence. Beat for 20 minutes at medium speed.

## LEMON BUTTERCREAM

Add the zest of 2 lemons and 30 ml (1 fl oz) lemon juice to the icing sugar and butter mixture. Beat for 5 minutes at medium speed before adding the eggs. Use only one teaspoon of essence. Beat for 20 minutes at medium speed.

## GERMAN BUTTERCREAM

*A light, sweet buttercream*

*300 g (10 ¹/₂ oz) unsalted butter*
*160 g (5 ¹/₂ oz) icing (powdered) sugar*
*200 ml (7 fl oz) milk*
*50 g (1 ³/₄ oz) caster (superfine) sugar*
*50 ml (1 ³/₄ fl oz) milk, extra*
*50 ml (1 ³/₄ oz) custard powder*
*4 x 60 g (2 oz, large) eggs*
*30 g (1 oz) caster (superfine) sugar, extra*

Beat the butter and icing sugar until light, fluffy and pale yellow.

Place the milk and caster sugar in a saucepan and bring to the boil. Blend the extra milk with the custard powder and eggs. Pour the hot milk over the custard mixture, stirring all the time. Return to the saucepan and cook over a medium heat until thickened. Do not allow to boil. Pour into a shallow dish, sprinkle with the extra caster sugar to prevent a skin from forming and chill quickly.

When the custard is cool, beat into the creamed butter and icing sugar a spoonful at a time. Beat for 10 minutes.

Makes 750 g (26 ¹/₂ oz)

## CHOCOLATE GERMAN BUTTERCREAM

Add 120 g (4 ¹/₄ oz) melted dark (plain or semi-sweet) chocolate to the hot custard mixture before chilling.

## ITALIAN BUTTERCREAM

*240 g (8 ¹/₂ oz) caster (superfine) sugar*
*100 ml (3 ¹/₂ fl oz) water*
*8 egg whites*
*400 g (14 oz) unsalted butter*

Place the sugar and water in a saucepan and bring to the boil. Cook until the temperature reaches 115 deg C (240 deg F), using a sugar (candy) thermometer. Beat the egg whites until soft peaks form and beat in the hot sugar syrup a little at a time. When all the syrup has been added, beat until the mixture is cold. Beat the butter until it is light and creamy and fold into the egg white mixture.

This very light buttercream is best used when fresh. It does not store well and reconstitution will not restore the light texture.

Makes 800 g (28 oz)

# CARAMEL

*500 g (17 ¹/₂ oz) caster (superfine) sugar*
*100 ml (3 ¹/₂ fl oz) water*
*1 level teaspoon glucose (corn) syrup*

Place all the ingredients in a saucepan and bring to the boil. When the mixture boils, wash down the sides of the saucepan with a pastry brush dipped in fresh clean water. Do not stir at any time. Using a sugar (candy) thermometer, boil until the mixture reaches a temperature of 160 deg C (320 deg F) when it will begin to brown. Remove from the heat immediately and dip the base of the saucepan in cold water for 4 seconds to prevent further cooking.

## CARAMEL THREADS

To make caramel threads, allow caramel to cool and thicken.

Cover the prongs of a fork with caramel. Allow the caramel to drip in a fine, continuous stream.

Using oiled fingers, pinch the bottom of the caramel stream and quickly pull away from the stream. Repeat until a collection of threads are held between the fingers.

Drape these threads over the cake to be decorated before making more threads.

**STEP ONE:** *Allow the caramel to drip in a fine, continuous stream.*

**STEP TWO:** *Collect the threads of caramel with oiled fingers.*

## PRALINE

*Praline is made by mixing caramel and almonds.*

*250 g (9 oz) caster (superfine) sugar*
*250 g (9 oz) flaked almonds*

Heat an empty heavy-based saucepan over medium heat. Slowly sprinkle the sugar into the pan and allow to melt before adding more. Keep adding the sugar slowly, stirring all the time. Heat until all the sugar has melted and is dark golden brown. Stir in the almonds.

For crushed praline, pour the mixture onto a 30 cm x 30 cm (12 in x 12 in) oiled sheet of aluminium foil. Spread using an oiled knife or palette knife. Allow to cool. When cold, crack into pieces and crush between two sheets of heavy plastic with a rolling pin.

Store in an airtight container.

To make a circle to cover the top of a cake, lightly oil a 30 cm x 30 cm (12 in x 12 in) sheet of aluminium foil. Place a lightly oiled cake ring on top of the foil. Pour the hot praline mixture into the ring and use an oiled knife to spread evenly.

When the edges of the praline have begun to cool, remove the ring. Use a warm, lightly oiled, large knife to cut the praline into the required portions. When cold remove from the oiled sheet and place on the top of the cake.

Makes sufficient praline to cover a Florentine Torte or, when crushed, a 23 cm (9 in) cake.

**STEP ONE:** *Stir the almonds into the caramel.*

**STEP TWO:** *Pour into a lightly oiled cake ring.*

**STEP THREE:** *Cut the praline while still warm.*

# CHOCOLATE

Two varieties of chocolate are used in this book: couverture chocolate and dark (plain or semi-sweet) chocolate.

Couverture chocolate is a pure form of chocolate which contains cocoa butter. If required for setting or moulding it needs to be prepared using a complicated and specialised process called tempering. For this reason, couverture chocolate is only used for its superior flavour and palatability and not for decoration.

Dark chocolate is more readily available and is made with vegetable fat instead of cocoa butter. This chocolate requires no special techniques and is used for coating cakes, making chocolate curls and collars and for piping.

## TO MELT CHOCOLATE

The easiest way to melt chocolate is in a double boiler or in a bowl over simmering water. Break the chocolate into small pieces to speed up the melting process.

Place a saucepan of water over the heat and bring to a simmer. Remove from the heat, place the chocolate into a small glass or stainless steel bowl which fits the saucepan and place the bowl over the hot water.

Never allow the water to come in contact with the bowl and stir the chocolate until it liquefies. Keep the chocolate liquefied while working. Place the bowl over simmering water in cold weather.

Melting or melted chocolate should never be covered as condensed water on the lid can fall back into the chocolate. Even a small amount of water in the melted chocolate will make it thicken and turn into a solid mass.

To cover a cake with chocolate, follow the method given in each recipe but always remember to work quickly and to spread the chocolate thinly.

To cover one 23 cm (9 in) cake, use 400 g (14 oz) of melted chocolate. If the chocolate is to be brushed over the cake, 300 g (10 $^{1}/_{4}$ oz) will be adequate.

# CHOCOLATE COLLARS

Chocolate collars add a special and decorative finish to any cake. Measure the height of the cake to be decorated and cut a strip of baking parchment one cm ($^1/_4$ in) higher than the cake and long enough to wrap around the circumference, approximately 25 cm (10 in). Spread 500 g (17 $^1/_2$ oz) of melted dark (plain or semi-sweet) chocolate over the strip of parchment paper.

As soon as the parchment is covered with chocolate pick it up lengthways by the top right and left hand corners and carefully wrap around the cake. Smooth the paper and chill for 5–10 minutes or until the collar is set. Carefully peel away the paper from the chocolate.

STEP THREE: *Remove the paper when the chocolate has set.*

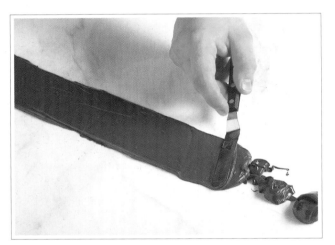

STEP ONE: *Spread melted chocolate onto a strip of baking parchment.*

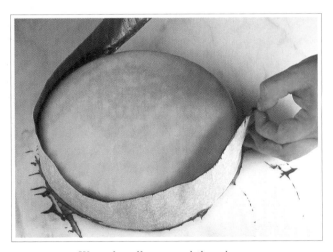

STEP TWO: *Wrap the collar around the cake.*

# PIPING CHOCOLATE

Before piping chocolate directly onto a cake, practise on a piece of parchment paper.

To pipe with chocolate, spoon a small amount of freshly melted dark (plain or semi-sweet) chocolate into a small paper piping (pastry) bag. Make sure no lumps are present. Fold over the ends of the bag. Cut the tip of the bag to the desired size.

Practise designs on parchment paper and allow to set. If desired, these designs can then be carefully peeled from the paper and placed on the cake.

# CHOCOLATE SHAVINGS

Pull a potato peeler smoothly and evenly across the surface. This will produce small shavings.

# CHOCOLATE SQUARES

*Decorate the top or sides of any cake with chocolate squares.*

**400 g (14 oz) dark (plain or semi-sweet) chocolate, melted**

Use a palette knife to spread the chocolate evenly onto a sheet of baking parchment 30 cm x 30 cm (12 in x 12 in). Leave in a cool place for 5–10 minutes to set. Mark 5 cm x 5 cm (2 in x 2 in) squares onto the chocolate and cut using a clean sharp knife. If the chocolate has begun to set hard, use a hot sharp knife.

Makes 20–30 chocolate squares.

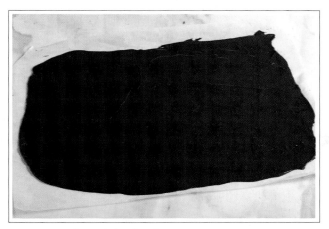

**STEP ONE:** *Spread the chocolate.*

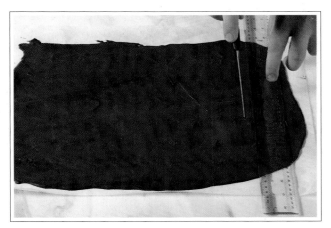

**STEP TWO:** *Mark into squares.*

**STEP THREE:** *Lift the squares when set hard.*

## CHOCOLATE CURLS

Pour melted dark (plain or semi-sweet) chocolate onto a marble slab or a stainless steel bench top (countertop) and use a palette knife to spread thinly. As the chocolate begins to set hold a large knife at a 45 degree angle to the bench top and pull gently through the chocolate. It is essential to work quickly or the chocolate will harden and splinter.

Approximately 500 g (17 ¹/₂ oz) of chocolate will make enough curls to cover a 23 cm (9 in) cake.

**STEP ONE:** *Spread the chocolate thinly.*

**STEP TWO:** *Pull a knife gently through the chocolate.*

## TWO-TONE CHOCOLATE CURLS

Pour melted white chocolate onto a marble slab or stainless steel bench top (countertop) and use a palette knife to spread thinly. Make one-way ridges with a comb scraper or fork. Allow to cool and harden. Pour melted dark (plain or semi-sweet) chocolate over the ridges of white chocolate. Spread thinly until the white chocolate is totally covered. As the chocolate begins to set pull a large knife with a blade at a 45 degree angle to the bench top through the chocolate.

**STEP ONE:** *Make one-way ridges in white chocolate.*

**STEP TWO:** *Pour melted dark chocolate over the hardened white chocolate.*

**STEP THREE:** *Pull a knife through the chocolate.*

## CHOCOLATE GONDOLAS

Draw a gondola shape onto a piece of parchment paper. Use a small amount of melted dark (plain or semi-sweet) chocolate in a piping (pastry) bag to pipe the outline of the object. Pipe between the lines to fill in the design. Leave the sheet in a cool place for 10 minutes to allow the design to set. Carefully peel the design from the paper.

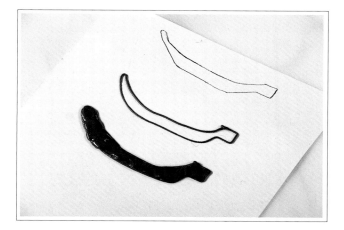

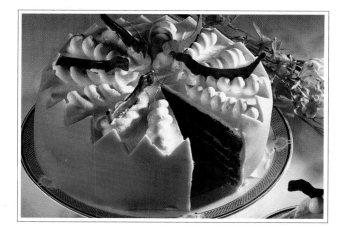

## MODELLING CHOCOLATE

*225 g (8 oz) glucose (corn) syrup*
*300 g (10 1/2 oz) chocolate, melted*

Place the syrup in a saucepan and heat until it liquefies. Remove from the heat and mix into the chocolate. Continue to stir until the mixture leaves the sides of the pan. Pour into a container lined with plastic (cling) wrap and allow to set at room temperature. Do not chill.

When the chocolate has set, roll out on a lightly floured bench (counter) until it is 3–4 mm (1/8 in) thick and fits the cake to be decorated. Stretch slightly and mould over the cake. Smooth the sides and allow any excess chocolate to drape over the centre of the cake. If the chocolate tears, tuck the torn area under and drape another piece over the torn area.

When the cake is completely covered dust lightly with cocoa powder.

Modelling chocolate will store in a cool dry place for up to 6 months.

Makes sufficient to cover one 23 cm (9 in) cake.

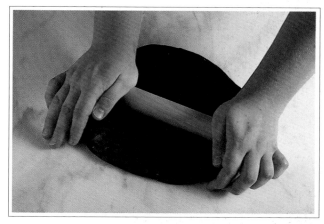

**STEP ONE:** *Roll out the chocolate.*

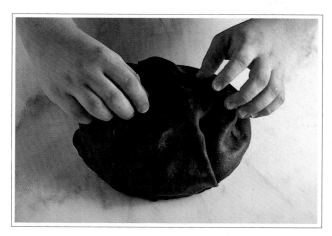

**STEP TWO:** *Drape over the cake.*

## GANACHE

*200 ml (7 fl oz) cream (single or light)*
*40 g (1 ¹/₂ oz) unsalted butter*
*600 g (21 oz) dark (plain or semi-sweet) chocolate,*
*chopped*

Place the cream and butter in a saucepan and bring to the boil. Add the chocolate and stir until melted.

The ganache can be used immediately to cover a cake. Place the cake on a wire rack and pour ganache over the entire cake. Use a palette knife to smooth the ganache and chill until set.

If the ganache is to be used as a whipped covering, allow to firm in a cool place. Whip with an electric mixer until lighter in colour.

## CONFECTIONER'S CUSTARD

*Set with gelatine, this custard is heavier than most.*

*250 ml (9 fl oz) cream (single or light)*
*250 ml (9 fl oz) milk*
*150 g (5 ¹/₄ oz) caster (superfine) sugar*
*75 ml (2 ³/₄ fl oz) milk, extra*
*90 ml (3 oz) cream (single or light), extra*
*75 g (2 ³/₄ oz) cornflour (cornstarch)*
*3 x 60 g (2 oz, large) eggs, lightly beaten*
*4 level teaspoons gelatine*
*30 ml (1 fl oz) water*

Place the cream, milk and sugar in a saucepan and bring to the boil. Remove from heat. Blend together the extra milk, extra cream, cornflour and eggs. Pour over the cold mixture, stirring all the time. Cook over a medium heat until the custard boils and thickens, stirring all the time.

Sprinkle the gelatine over the water in a small bowl and soak for 5–10 minutes. Stand in a pan of hot water until the gelatine is dissolved. Mix into the hot custard. Sprinkle the surface of the hot custard with caster sugar to prevent a skin from forming or place greased greaseproof (waxed) paper directly on the custard.

Allow the custard to cool or use according to the recipe.

Makes approximately 900 ml (32 fl oz) custard.

## CRÈME CHANTILLY

*600 ml (21 fl oz) cream (single or light), well chilled*
*100 g (3 ¹/₂ oz) icing (powdered) sugar, sifted*
*1 teaspoon vanilla essence (extract)*

Place all the ingredients in a mixing bowl and beat until the mixture forms stiff peaks. Chill.

Makes sufficient to cover a 23 cm (9 in) cake.

## CRÈME CHIBOUST

*A very light custard set with gelatine and blended with Italian meringue.*

*4 level teaspoons gelatine*
*60 ml (2 fl oz) water*
*150 ml (5 ¹/₄ fl oz) orange juice*
*125 ml (4 ¹/₂ fl oz) cream*
*45 g (1 ¹/₂ oz) caster (superfine) sugar*
*60 g (2 oz) cornflour (cornstarch)*
*6 egg yolks*
*6 egg whites*
*210 g (7 ¹/₂ oz) caster (superfine) sugar, extra*
*30 ml (1 fl oz) water, extra*

Sprinkle the gelatine over the water in a small bowl and soak for 5–10 minutes. Stand in a pan of hot water until the gelatine is dissolved. Place the juice and cream in a saucepan and bring to the boil. Remove from heat and pour into a mixing bowl. Beat the sugar, cornflour and egg yolks together and pour onto the hot cream and juice, whisking all the time. Return the mixture to the saucepan and cook over a medium heat until thickened. Cool slightly and stir in the dissolved gelatine. Cool.

Place the extra sugar and water in a saucepan and bring to the boil. Cook until the temperature reaches 130 deg C (266 deg F) using a sugar (candy) thermometer. Beat the egg whites until stiff peaks form (see page 173) and pour onto the hot syrup. Beat until the mixture is cold. Gently fold in by hand the cooled custard. Use immediately.

Crème Chiboust cannot be stored as it cannot be reconstituted from a cold state. If a small amount is left over, try to spread it over the cake.

Makes sufficient to decorate one cake. If a high cake is desired, e.g. the Chocolate Herrison Torte, adjust the recipe to make one and a half times the original quantity.

# CRÈME PÂTISSIÈRE

*A sweet, light boiled custard.*

*250 ml (9 fl oz) milk*
*250 ml (9 fl oz) cream (single or light)*
*125 g (4 1/2 oz) caster (superfine) sugar*
*75 ml (2 3/4 fl oz) milk, extra*
*75 ml (2 3/4 fl oz) cream, extra*
*100 g (3 1/2 oz) cornflour (cornstarch)*
*2 x 60 g (2 oz, large) eggs, lightly beaten*

Place the milk, cream and sugar in a saucepan and bring to the boil. Blend together the extra milk, extra cream, cornflour and eggs and pour onto the hot mixture, stirring all the time. Cook over a medium heat until the custard boils and thickens, stirring all the time. Remove from the heat and scrape down the sides of the saucepan. Allow to cool at room temperature or use according to recipe instructions.

To prevent a skin from forming on the cooling custard, sprinkle a small amount of caster sugar over the surface. This will dissolve and form a syrup which can be whisked into the custard after cooling. Alternatively, place a sheet of greased greaseproof (waxed) paper directly on top of the custard.

Makes sufficient for a single recipe, approximately 900 ml (32 fl oz).

Crème Pâtissière can be stored in an airtight container in the refrigerator for 3–4 days.

# FROSTINGS

*A frosting is a sweet icing which should form a slightly hard, thin crust on the outside and be soft on the inside.*

*500 g (17 1/2 oz) icing (powdered) sugar, sifted*
*40 g (1 1/2 oz) glucose (corn) syrup*
*60 g (2 oz) unsalted butter*
*60 ml (2 fl oz) water*
*1 teaspoon vanilla essence (extract)*

Place the butter, icing sugar and glucose in a mixing bowl and blend slowly.

When all the ingredients are thoroughly mixed, slowly add the water and vanilla a little at a time and mix thoroughly after each addition. When all the ingredients are blended, beat for 15 minutes at top speed until the frosting is white, light and fluffy.

STORAGE: Always keep the frosting covered with a damp cloth or store in an airtight container.

Makes sufficient to cover one 23 cm (9 in) cake.

# LEMON OR ORANGE FROSTING

*rind and juice of 2 lemons or 2 oranges*
*550 g (19 1/2 oz) icing (powdered) sugar, sifted*
*40 g (1 1/2 oz) glucose (corn) syrup*
*60 g (2 oz) unsalted butter*

Place the rind, icing sugar, syrup and butter in a mixing bowl and blend slowly. When ingredients are combined, add the juice slowly, stirring all the time. When all ingredients are thoroughly mixed, beat for 15 minutes at top speed or until the frosting is white, light and fluffy.

Makes sufficient to cover one 23 cm (9 in) cake.

## CHOCOLATE FROSTING

*60 g (2 oz) cocoa powder*
*500 g (17 1/2 oz) icing (powdered) sugar, sifted*
*40 g (1 1/2 oz) glucose (corn) syrup*
*75 g (2 1/2 oz) unsalted butter*
*60 ml (2 fl oz) water*

Place the cocoa powder, icing sugar, syrup and butter in a mixing bowl and blend slowly. When combined, add the water slowly, beating all the time. When all the ingredients are combined, beat for 15 minutes at top speed until the frosting is light and fluffy.

Makes sufficient to cover one 23 cm (9 in) cake.

## CREAM CHEESE FROSTING

*Classified as a frosting because it is so light, this variation does not form a crust when exposed to the air.*

*400 g (14 oz) icing (powdered) sugar*
*150 g (5 1/4 oz) cream cheese, softened*
*100 g (3 1/2 oz) unsalted butter, softened*
*1 teaspoon vanilla essence (extract)*
*30 ml (1 fl oz) milk*

Place icing sugar, cream cheese and butter into a mixing bowl and combine.

Add the vanilla essence and milk and mix at top speed for 5 minutes or until light and fluffy.

Makes sufficient to cover one 23 cm (9 in) cake.

**STORAGE:** Make frosting only when required. Always store any surplus mixture in an airtight container in the refrigerator. Never store for more than 10–14 days or taste and texture will be affected.

## LEMON OR ORANGE CREAM CHEESE FROSTING

To produce a lemon or orange flavoured Cream Cheese Frosting, add the rind of two oranges or two lemons and replace the milk with freshly squeezed juice.

Follow the method described in the rest of the recipe.

# GLAZES

## FONDANT GLAZE

For the small amounts required it is more convenient to buy fondant. Most large supermarkets and delicatessens stock ready-made fondant in small tubs. If fondant is not available, use water icing.

To melt fondant, place in a small bowl over a pan of simmering water. If it is too stiff to spread easily, add a very small amount of water. Do not heat above 30 deg C (86 deg F) or the fondant will crystallize.

To store fondant, keep covered with a thin layer of water or sugar syrup to prevent it forming a skin and drying out.

## APRICOT GLAZE

*250 g (9 oz) apricot jam*
*60 ml (2 fl oz) water*
*2 teaspoons lemon juice*

Place all the ingredients in a saucepan and stir until thoroughly blended and smooth. Boil for 10–15 minutes. Force through a fine wire strainer. Brush the warm glaze over the cake. Allow to cool before decorating.

Store excess glaze in a covered container in the refrigerator. Do not store for more than 3 weeks.

Makes sufficient to cover one 23 cm (9 in) cake.

## STRAWBERRY GLAZE

*250 g (9 oz) strawberry jam*
*60 ml (2 fl oz) water*
*2 teaspoons lemon juice*

Place all the ingredients in a saucepan and stir until blended and smooth. Boil for 10–15 minutes. Force through a fine wire strainer. Brush the warm glaze over the cake. Allow to cool before decorating the cake.

Store excess glaze in a covered container in the refrigerator. Do not store for more than 3 weeks.

Makes sufficient to cover one 23 cm (9 in) cake.

## SACHER TORTE GLAZE

*250 g (9 oz) caster (superfine) sugar*
*200 g (7 oz) couverture chocolate, chopped*
*150 ml (5 fl oz) water*

Place all the ingredients into a saucepan and slowly bring to the boil.

Boil until the syrup reaches 115 deg C (240 deg F), using a sugar (candy) thermometer. Cool slightly and pour over the apricot glazed torte.

One quantity of this mixture will cover one cake.

## EGG WASH

*Egg Wash gives a glossy sheen to cakes and is also used to join and seal layers of pastry before baking.*

*1 x 60 g (2 oz, large) egg*
*30 ml (1 fl oz) water*

Lightly beat the egg. Mix in the water. The Egg Wash is now ready to use.

Makes sufficient to glaze the top of any cake.

Egg Wash can be stored in a covered container in the refrigerator for 2 days.

# ICINGS

## ROYAL ICING

*Traditionally used to decorate wedding cakes, Royal Icing can also be used for small decorations and writing and to cover elaborate cakes. This icing dries out easily and must be covered at all times with a slightly damp cloth. If the icing forms a skin or crust, small lumps will block the piping (pastry) bag nozzle when trying to write.*

*1 egg white, at room temperature*
*350 g (12 1/4 oz) icing (powdered) sugar, sifted*
*1–2 drops of acetic acid or lemon juice*

Place the egg white in a small bowl. Add 2 teaspoons of the icing sugar and beat for 2 minutes by hand or until mixture is combined. Stir in the acetic acid or lemon juice. Add the remaining icing sugar a spoonful at a time, beating well after each addition.

Add enough icing sugar to reach the 'soft peak' stage, when the icing mixture can hold a peak and fold back down (see page 173). At this stage, the icing is suitable for writing and lattice work.

To make shell borders and piped flowers, add more icing sugar to form firm peaks. At this stage the icing mixture will hold peaks when flecked upwards (see page 173).

To store the icing, place it in a plastic bag inside a plastic container to prevent drying out and setting. Do not store for more than 3 days and beat for 5–10 minutes before using.

To cover a cake with Royal Icing, place a thin layer of rolled marzipan over the cake then spread the icing over the top and sides. Royal Icing can be smoothed before decorating or use a palette knife to fleck the icing to form small peaks.

The cake should be eaten within 2–3 days or the icing will dry out and become hard.

## WATER ICING

*500 g (17 1/2 oz) icing (powdered) sugar*
*warm water*

Mix the icing sugar with sufficient water to make an icing thick enough to leave a trail when it is swirled over itself. It has to remain thin enough to spread.

Makes approximately 600 g (21 oz), sufficient to cover one 23 cm (9 in) cake.

## FEATHERING

Feathering uses water icing, fondant or chocolate to produce effective decorations on any cake.

Cover the top surface of the cake with a thin layer of the desired topping and smooth. Pipe different coloured topping in lines or circles over the first layer. Draw a toothpick or knife through the toppings from one side of the cake to the other. When 6–7 lines have been drawn in one direction, turn the cake around and repeat the process.

Approximately 200 g (7 oz) of (e.g.) fondant is sufficient to decorate one 23 cm (9 in) cake.

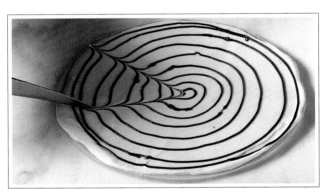

## MARZIPAN

Also known as almond paste, marzipan is a sweetened mixture of ground (minced) almonds, glucose (corn) syrup and icing (powdered) sugar. It is often the first layer used to cover highly decorated cakes. Marzipan is available in a variety of sizes and packagings, from 200 g (7 oz) rolls to 7 kg (15 1/2 lb) boxes and is white or yellow depending on the manufacturer's recipe.

Marzipan covered cakes will not dry out when stored for long periods of time.

**STORAGE:** Marzipan can absorb moisture or dry out so careful storage is important. If it absorbs moisture it will begin to dissolve. If marzipan dries out it will begin to ferment.

Wrap in plastic (cling) wrap and place in an airtight container. Store at room temperature in a dark place for up to 3 weeks.

**TO COVER A CAKE:** To cover a 23 cm (9 in) cake, roll out 500 g (17 1/2 oz) of marzipan on a floured bench (counter) 3–4 cm (1–1 1/2 in) wider than the top of the cake. This will cover the top and sides of the cake.

The cake will have been covered with a cream or glaze. Slide both hands underneath the piece of marzipan to pick it up. Place in the centre of the cake slowly, letting it fall from your hands as you pull them away.

Smooth the top and sides of the marzipan to remove any air bubbles and stretch downwards to fit. If air bubbles remain, prick carefully with a toothpick or pin to expel the air.

**BAKING WITH MARZIPAN:** To bake marzipan it must have a *higher* proportion of almonds than sugar. If the proportion of sugar is too high, the marzipan will boil instead of bake and this will adversely affect the finished cake.

**NOTE:** *This rule does not apply to the Simnel Cake.*

**TO TINT MARZIPAN:** It is often easier to achieve a realistic appearance by using untinted marzipan for modelling and painting the finished product when it is dry.

To tint marzipan, flatten the piece to be coloured and add a drop of food colouring to the centre. Fold the marzipan to enclose the colouring. Lightly knead the marzipan until the colouring is completely absorbed. Continue to add food colouring drop by drop until the required colour is achieved.

## MARZIPAN BANANAS

Roll a small piece of yellow tinted marzipan in the palm of your hand until it forms a ball.

Roll into a sausage shape. Slight pressure on one side while rolling will taper the sausage. Place the tapered sausage shape onto a bench top (countertop) and bend to resemble a banana. Square off by pinching the thickest end between three fingers.

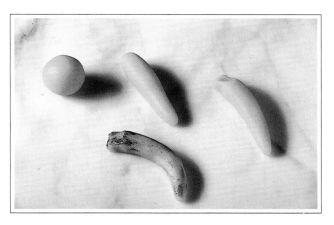

Use the back of a spoon or knife to smooth the curved surface of the banana. Allow to dry for one hour before painting with green food colouring and melted dark (plain or semi-sweet) chocolate.

Approximately 300 g (10 ½ oz) of marzipan will make 12 bananas.

These can be made before baking the cake and stored for up to 3 weeks in a covered airtight container. If required for display only they will keep for 6 months uncovered.

## MARZIPAN CARROTS

Roll a small piece of orange tinted marzipan between the palms of the hands until it forms a ball.

Roll back and forth to taper the ball at one end. The narrow end should be short and blunt, not pointed.

Place the carrot on a bench top (countertop) and use the back of a knife to score light marks all over the carrot.

Approximately 250 g (9 oz) of marzipan will make 12 carrots.

These can be made before baking the cake and can be stored for up to 3 weeks in an airtight container. If required for display only they will keep for 6 months uncovered.

## MARZIPAN LEAVES

Roll a small piece of green tinted marzipan between the palms of the hands to form a ball. Roll between the base of the hands to taper one end. One end should be pointed.

Place the tapered marzipan onto a bench top (countertop) and flatten two sides to shape a leaf, leaving a central vein.

Use a sharp knife to remove the leaf from the bench and mark veins down the sloping sides.

Approximately 200 g (7 oz) of marzipan will make 12 leaves.

These can be made before baking the cake and stored for up to 3 weeks in an airtight container. If required for display only they can be kept for 6 months uncovered.

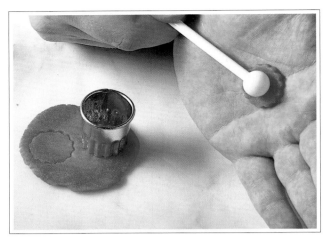

**STEP ONE:** *Cut out shapes using a fluted cutter.*

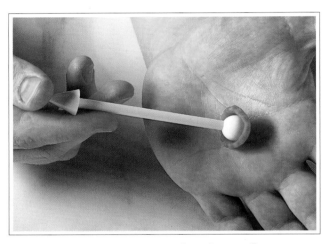

**STEP TWO:** *Use a marzipan tool to shape a flower.*

## MARZIPAN FLOWERS

Roll out a small piece of tinted marzipan to a thickness of 2 mm ($^1/_{16}$ in). Cut out required shapes using a fluted round cutter.

Place a piece of marzipan in the palm of the hand and use a marzipan tool or a smooth round object to shape a flower. Only a slight amount of pressure is needed. The marzipan will curl at the edges to form a flower.

Approximately 150 g (5 $^1/_4$ oz) of marzipan will make 12 flowers. These can be made before baking the cake and stored for up to 3 weeks in an airtight container. If required for display only they can be kept for 6 months uncovered.

**STEP THREE:** *Marzipan flower.*

## MARZIPAN HOLLY AND BERRIES

Roll out a small piece of green tinted marzipan to a thickness of 2 mm ($^1/_{16}$ in).

Use a holly shaped cutter or a plain round cutter and small, sharp knife to cut the holly leaf. Roll small pieces of red tinted marzipan into balls for the holly spray.

These can be made before baking the cake and can be stored for up to 3 weeks in an airtight container. If required for display only they will keep for 6 months uncovered.

# ROASTED FLAKED ALMONDS

*Simple and quick to make, roasted slivered almonds are a great side decoration for any cake.*

### 250 g (9 oz) flaked almonds

Preheat oven to 180 deg C (350 deg F). Spread the almonds thinly on a baking tray (sheet). Bake for 4 minutes. Remove the tray and use a fork to turn the almonds. Return to oven and bake for a further 4 minutes. Remove and turn again. Continue this process until the almonds are golden brown. Allow to cool on the tray.

When cold, press the almonds around the sides of a cake covered with glaze or cream.

Makes sufficient to cover the sides of one 23 cm (9 in) cake. Roasted almonds can be stored in an airtight container for up to 2 weeks.

# IMPORTANT NOTES

In all cake recipes the author prefers salted butter. In sweet recipes such as buttercreams and frostings use unsalted butter. Salt can be added to the sweeter recipes to suit personal tastes.

In recipes which use only half of a cooked sponge do not throw away the other half. All left over sponge can be frozen in a sealed container and used in recipes which require cake crumbs.

All ingredients should be at room temperature when used unless the recipe advises otherwise.

Ensure that all utensils are clean, grease free and dry before cooking. Water or grease on utensils can adversely affect recipes, especially when using egg whites which will not achieve maximum aeration if mixed with even small amounts of water or grease.

## MIXED SPICE

*1 level teaspoon ground cinnamon*
*¹/₂ level teaspoon ground ginger*
*¹/₄ level teaspoon ground nutmeg*
*¹/₄ level teaspoon ground cloves*

Combine all dry ingredients in a small mixing bowl.

## RIBBON STAGE

The 'ribbon stage' of any mixture has been achieved when a dribble from the whisk or spoon will form an impression of itself on top of the mixture and remain there for the count of 8 or indefinitely.

## YEAST

Fresh compressed yeast is preferable for all recipes. However, it is possible to use dried yeast. 14 g (¹/₂ oz) of dried yeast is equivalent to 30 g (1 oz) of fresh yeast. If using dried yeast add the flour and dry ingredients and then add liquid to the combined ingredients.

## OVEN TEMPERATURES AND GAS MARKS

The following two tables give the equivalent Numbered Temperature Control Knob Setting for gas ovens. Check the temperature (given in degrees Celsius) in the appropriate table for your oven.

100 degrees C — ¹/₄
110 degrees C — ¹/₂
120 degrees C — 1
140 degrees C — 2
150 degrees C — 3
160 degrees C — 4
180 degrees C — 5
190 degrees C — 6
200 degrees C — 7
220 degrees C — 8
230 degrees C — 9

100 degrees C — 1
110 degrees C — 2
120 degrees C — 3
140 degrees C — 4
150 degrees C — 5
160 degrees C — 6
180 degrees C — 7
190 degrees C — 8
200 degrees C — 9
220 degrees C — 10
230 degrees C — 11
250 degrees C — 12

Courtesy of the Australian Gas Cooking School.

## CONVERSIONS

Metric and imperial units are given for all ingredient quantities. The nearest imperial equivalent has been provided in all cases. Small differences in metric units have been absorbed (eg 125 g and 130 g are both converted to 4 ¹/₂ oz) and will not affect the recipe.

# EGG WHITES

## SOFT PEAKS

Beaten egg whites reach the soft peak stage when the peaks will slowly fold back down on the count of four.

## STIFF PEAKS

The stiff peak stage has been reached when the peaks will hold their shape indefinitely.

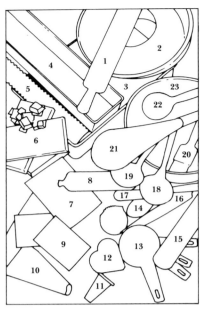

## Equipment

1. basket-weave rolling pin.
2. savarin ring (ring mold)
3. baking tray (sheet)
4. bar/loaf tin
5. grooved rolling pin
6. cooking chocolate (couverture)
7. custard powder
8. marzipan/almond paste
9. baking powder
10. piping bag (pastry bag)
11. nozzle for piping bag
12. biscuit (cookie) cutters
13. measuring cups
14. marzipan leaf mould
15. large palette knife
16. knife
17. small palette knife
18. sieved spoon
19. ladle
20. pastry brush
21. fine wire whisk
22. sieve
23. 23 cm (9 in) spring form cake pan

# INDEX